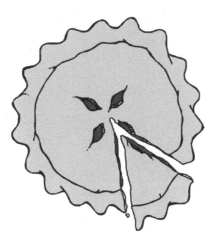

Slicing Pie
HANDBOOK

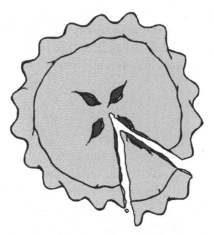

Slicing Pie

HANDBOOK

Perfect Equity Splits for Startups

Mike Moyer

Foreword by Noam Wasserman

Lake
Shark

ISBN 978-0692584620

This publication is designed to provide accurate and authoritative information regarding the subject matter covered. It is sold with the understanding that the publisher is not engaged in rendering legal, accounting, or other professional services. If legal advice or other expert assistance is required, the services of a competent professional person should be sought.—*From a Declaration of Principles Jointly Adopted by a Committee of the American Bar Association and a Committee of Publishers and Associations*

All brand names and product names used in this book are trademarks, registered trademarks, or trade names of their respective holders. I wonder if anyone ever reads this page.

Published by Lake Shark Ventures, LLC
Lake Forest, IL
www.LakeShark.com

This book belongs to:

_____

Working for this company (the Pie):

_____

With a fair-market salary of:

_____

Our Pie uses the following numbers in the *Slicing Pie* calculations:

Non-cash multiplier:	
Cash multiplier:	
Royalty for ideas:	%
Commission on sales:	%
Investor finder's fee:	%
Loyal employee protection:	○ months ○ %
Personal car:	○ cash ○ non-cash ○ split

(This will make more sense once you've read the book!)

The Slicing Pie Principle

% share of the *reward* = % share of what's *at risk*

My Promise

If, after reading this book, you don't feel that it contains not just good advice, but the greatest advice on the subject that you have ever received, I will happily refund your money and apologize for wasting your time.

Mike@SlicingPie.com

My Butt-Covering Disclaimer

If anything in this book sounds like legal advice — it's not. If anything in this book sounds like financial advice — it's not. I'm not a lawyer and I'm not an accountant, and I'm not a certified financial advisor.

I'm just a guy who wants you, and your teammates, to get what you deserve from your startup. No more and no less!

Foreword

"Don't shake that hand!" That was my reaction in 2008 when I first saw the results of the equity-split analyses I was doing with Thomas Hellmann.[1] I had seen the problems personally time after time with founding teams, but now had systematic evidence across more than a thousand U.S. startups: The most common ways in which founders split the equity were also the most hazardous.

In particular, we found that 73% of teams split the equity within the first month of the startup, at the heights of the uncertainty about their startup's strategy and business model, their roles in it, and their levels of commitment to it. Most of the teams barely spent any time discussing the split, avoiding having the difficult conversations necessary to really understand each other's potential contributions and intentions. And the majority of them split it statically – i.e., didn't

---

[1] The final version of the paper with those analyses is Hellmann, T. & N. Wasserman (2016) The first deal: The division of founder equity in new ventures. *Management Science*.

allow for future adjustments as new information emerged about contributions and commitment.

I started referring to teams who had split equally without much discussion as "Quick Handshake" teams. Our analyses showed that Quick Handshake teams incurred a significant penalty when raising their first round of financing, either in reduced ability to raise the round or in lower average valuations if they did raise, *ceteris paribus*. And that was only the cost in terms of financing; within the founding teams themselves, the destructive tensions caused by a bad split are often even more devastating.

If you're in the early days of a founding journey and your cofounder proposes a Quick Handshake – maybe "to get it out of the way" so you can focus on "what really counts" – don't succumb to those pressures. Even a startup with a great idea can be stopped in its tracks by such a decision. Zipcar succeeded despite the fact that founder-CEO Robin Chase suffered "years of angst" due to her Quick Handshake. Likewise, for Facebook with Mark Zuckerberg's ill-considered static split with Eduardo Saverin, which caused costly legal fisticuffs between the cofounders.

For every startup like these that survives a disastrous equity split, many more fail because of it. In fact, how founders split the equity among themselves is one of the biggest make-or-break issues they face as a team.[2] Make sure that your equity-split decisions will heighten your chances of success rather than imperil them. Don't succumb to the rosy expectations that pervade the entrepreneurial mindset during the early days when Robin and Zuck split the equity, when they were least likely to anticipate, discuss, and plan for pitfalls on their journey.

How can founders avoid the angst, destructive tension, and legal problems that come with a bad equity split? Robin Chase's hard-learned advice was to adopt something more "organic" – something that takes seriously the remaining uncertainties and is able to adjust to their occurrence. The most common "organic" approach is to adopt vesting, in which the individual has to earn his or her equity stake instead of being granted it fully at the time of the split. In the U.S., this vesting is almost always time-based, but about 10% of teams adopt milestone-based vesting, which requires clearly-definable milestones, a concrete division of labor within the team, and other characteristics lacking in many founding teams. Vesting is a huge improvement over the static splits that pervade Founderdom. However, in many cases, time is a

---

[2] As a whole, I call those make-or-break issues the "3Rs": The founders' prior Relationships, the ways they allocate the Roles and decision making within the team, and the allocation of Rewards.[2] Across the 3Rs, the most pervasive theme is that founders' most common decisions tend to be the ones that are the most fraught with peril. For more on the 3Rs, see Chapters 4-7 of Wasserman, N. 2012. *The Founder's Dilemmas: Anticipating and Avoiding the Pitfalls That Can Sink a Startup.* Princeton, NJ: Princeton University Press.

weak proxy for the creation of value in a startup, making it an imperfect basis on which to split.

Over the last four years, I've been delighted to see the impact that Mike Moyer has had on the spread of dynamic approaches to splitting equity. After years of road-testing it, he has honed an approach to equity splits that educates founders about the perils identified in my research, gives them a framework for adopting dynamism, and provides them with the tools to execute his style of dynamic splits.

Please consider seriously the types of risks you face, have a serious conversation about them with your cofounders, and then see if Mike's approach to slicing the pie might help you prepare for one of the key pitfalls that can sink a startup.

Dr. Noam Wasserman
Founding Director, Founder Central initiative at the University of Southern California
Author, *The Founder's Dilemmas: Anticipating and Avoiding the Pitfalls That Can Sink a Startup*

Contents

Chapter One:

Meet Slicing Pie

My mission in life is to make sure that every entrepreneur on the planet gets what they deserve from their company.

We live in a world where entrepreneurs and early-stage company participants get taken advantage of so frequently that we hardly notice. Bad equity deals are the rule, not the exception. Fairness is rare. The *intent* for fairness is there, but the *practice* of fairness is not. *Slicing Pie* (aka "Grunt Fund") is an equity model that allows people to align their *intent* of being fair with their *ability* to actually pull it off.

I'm going to start off with a high-level overview of the *Slicing Pie* model before jumping in to the nitty-gritty of how it works. Once you get your head around the concept, it will make plenty of sense, but it's not conventional wisdom. The conventional wisdom, as you shall see, has major flaws. But, you may already know this if you're struggling with equity splits for your startup. By the time you finish reading, you will know *exactly* how to split up the equity in your company.

Slicing Pie a straightforward process for implementing a "*dynamic*", or "*organic*" equity split in an early-stage startup that ensures the fairest equity split possible. It is designed for bootstrapped startups and is used *prior* to cash flow breakeven or the first major funding event.

It is a universal, one-size-fits-all, self-adjusting model that maintains fairness even as things change. Startup companies change all the time. People come and go, strategies change, cash is consumed (when it's available), and every day people contribute more to the company's success. The only thing that *doesn't* change about startups is the fact that they are always changing.

Startup Equity

Equity in a startup entitles the owner to a portion of the company's rewards, if and when they come. The rewards are a portion of the future profits or the proceeds of a sale.

Slicing Pie is based on a simple principle: **a person's % share of the rewards should *always* be equal to that person's % share of what's put at risk to attain those rewards.**

When a person contributes to a startup company and does not get paid for their contribution, they are putting their contribution *at risk* with the *hopes* of getting a future reward. And, while the timing and the amount of the future reward is unknowable, the amount of the contributions at-risk *is* knowable. *It is equal to the fair market value of the contributions.*

Because it's *impossible* to know when or even if the rewards will ever come, we can never know how much people must put at risk to get the rewards. Every contribution, therefore, is essentially a *bet* on the future of the company and nobody knows when the betting will end.

Blackjack

Think of the startup as a game of Blackjack. You and a partner each bet $1 on the *same* hand. You have no way of knowing if you're going to win or even how much you're going to win as different hands pay different amounts. The future, in other words, is *un*knowable. What *is* knowable is that you each contributed the same amount and that amount is at-risk because you could lose it all.

If you win, you should split the winnings 50/50, which is perfectly fair because you each bet the same.

But, what if the dealer deals two Aces? You didn't expect this, and you want to take advantage of the new opportunity, so you decide split the Aces and double-down. (If you don't know how to play Blackjack, "splitting the Aces" means you are turning one hand into two hands and placing another bet.) Unfortunately, your partner is out of money. You aren't, so you bet $2 more. Again, you have no way of knowing if you're going to win or how much you're going to win. What you *do* know is that you bet $3 and your partner bet $1.

Does 50/50 still seem like a fair deal? Probably not. In this scenario you deserve 75% of the winnings because you placed 75% of the bets. This is the essence of the *Slicing Pie* model.

If you simply keep track of what people bet, you can calculate *exactly* what portion of the rewards they deserve. It's quite simple!

A Dynamic Model

Slicing Pie is *dynamic* model because it changes over time. This is because every day brings more bets of time, expenses, facilities, supplies and anything else the company needs to move forward. Keeping track of these things takes a little discipline, but it's not a huge deal and the benefits are enormous.

When you apply the *Slicing Pie* model, each person will get *exactly* what they deserve to get—including you. From the moment you start working with a *Slicing Pie* startup, you begin to accrue your share of the Pie. Your interests will be *perfectly* aligned with the other members of the team, so if you like the team and the business, you can rest assured that your money, time or other contributions will be handled with perfect fairness. If you don't like the team, you can leave and the termination rules (mentioned below) kick in and everyone is still happy.

A New Mental Model for Equity Splits

Slicing Pie represents a new way of thinking about equity. It challenges the traditional thinking around equity splits because traditional models don't work. People try to make them work, but they never, ever produce a fair result. Here's why traditional models don't work:

The Fixed-Split Problem

Traditionally, nearly every startup company uses a pre-negotiated "*fixed*" or "*static*" equity split. In a fixed split, equity is doled out to participants in chunks, based on their *potential* contribution. This is kind of like paying someone their annual salary on their first day of work because they told their manager they were going to work hard. If it sounds silly, it is, but it happens all the time because many entrepreneurs *believe they can predict the future*. In fact, if they *don't* believe they can predict the future they probably wouldn't have the confidence to start a company in the first place. Optimism and confidence are important, but they don't give anyone special powers like seeing the future.

So, with the best intentions, founders enter into fixed equity split agreements loosely based on their predictions of this equation:

$$\text{Your Share \%} = \frac{\text{The Value of Your Contribution}}{\text{The Total Value}}$$

This is easy if they know what the numbers are. For instance, if a you invested $100,000 in a company that has a post-money valuation of $1,000,000 you would have 10%:

$$10\% = \frac{\$100,000}{\$1,000,000}$$

This is perfectly fair. You get a percentage that is in proportion to what you contributed. In most cases, however, we *don't* know the values because they are likely to change, so people try to *predict/estimate/guess* the variables.

Founders have to predict the *future* value of each person's contribution (aka the economic benefit to the firm) and they have to predict the total *future* value of the firm (because the current value is most likely $0). Both of the answers to these questions will no doubt be based on a complex set of assumptions with virtually no grounding in reality.

Try as they might, their numbers will be wild guesses at best. At worst, they will be overly optimistic fantasies of a meteoric rise to fame and fortune. It's *impossible* to create a fair fixed equity split. And even if they could, a split that was right one day will be wrong the next because startups always change. It's such a complicated, emotionally-charged discussion that many founders either avoid it altogether or do an even split like 50/50 or 25/25/25/25.

All Splits Are Dynamic

Sooner or later, *all* splits will need be adjusted. In traditional equity models, the split often adjusts— incorrectly—after some kind of founder conflict. The adjustments simply set the team up for another fight later on—I call it the "Fix & Fight" model.

What Might Change

You may wonder what could possibly change to cause such founder conflict. The answer is *everything*. Whatever you *think* you and your partners will commit in terms of time, money, ideas, relationships, facilities, supplies or anything else will likely be different as the company actually unfolds. When things change, you'll be faced with one of two realities:

The first possible reality is that your share is *less* than you deserve.

$$\text{Your Share \%} < \frac{\text{The Value of Your Contribution}}{\text{The Total Value}}$$

This is probably *not* okay with you. If you have *less* than you deserve, it means there is someone out there who has *more* than they deserve and they got it at *your* personal expense. The greater the personal expense, the more upsetting this will be. You might even try to figure out who got *more* than their fair share and try to get some back with your posse of highly-paid attorneys (if you can afford them). This happens all the time. (Have you seen the *Facebook* movie?)

Even if you *agreed* to this arrangement in advance it's still not fair. The only reason people agree to this kind of treatment is if they had no other choice or if they didn't know any better. This, too, happens all the time. Some people have a habit of taking advantage of other people when they sense desperation or ignorance.

If you've ever been caught on the short end of this equation (as many of us have) you are probably going to try to avoid this situation in the future by making sure you cover your own butt. The greater the pain you endured, the greater your interest will be in covering your own butt, even if it means someone else has to lose. This leads us to the second reality that is also *not* fair:

$$\text{Your Share \%} > \frac{\text{The Value of Your Contribution}}{\text{The Total Value}}$$

In this case you have *more* than you deserve. In many cases the more money, knowledge or power one person has over the other person, the greater their share will be at the expense of the other.

This may be okay with you if you are comfortable with the fact that someone else, who deserved more, had to take less so that you could have more than you deserved. I hope this is not you. If this *is* you then *Slicing Pie* isn't for you and you should *not* participate in a company that uses it. There are plenty of other opportunities out there for you to take advantage of people. I know this is harsh, but I don't think it's okay to take advantage of others.

I am an advocate of fairness. I believe that every person deserves what they deserve. No more and no less. I don't want to work with people who want to take advantage of me or others, and I don't want to take advantage of others myself. I want to reward the people who help me get to where I'm going.

Given the current startup funding landscape, fairness is hard to achieve. We live in a world where it is so common for people to take advantage of one another that they may not even realize they are doing it!

Not everyone is comfortable with fairness and transparency. That's okay, but please don't try to force them to use a different model; fairness is too important. Just walk away.

Alligator Pits

Because fixed equity splits stop being fair the moment something changes, nearly every startup has less-than alligators (<) representing people who have *less* than they deserve, and greater-than alligators (>) representing people who have *more* than they deserve. Eventually, the less-than people will get upset and want to renegotiate. Everyone becomes poised for a fight. I call these "Alligator Pit" negotiations.

Less Than Gator   Greater Than Gator

In a fixed equity split, *every* negotiation is an alligator pit because sooner or later something will change and it will stop being fair.

When we approach the alligator pit, we do it with fear, mistrust and a keen instinct towards self-preservation. These are not the best building blocks for creating an awesome company.

Every time something changes, founders have to jump back in the alligator pit and *re*negotiate. Things *always* change, so it's always a big, bloody frenzy of gnashing teeth and swinging tails. This happens over and over again and each session in the alligator pit weakens working relationships. It's a nightmare.

In an effort to protect ourselves from the snarling alligators that gnash their teeth and swing their tails, we invent concepts like vesting, oppressive liquidation preferences and the dreaded full-ratchet anti-dilution. Our attempts to protect ourselves from the alligator pits are expensive, time consuming, and often exacerbate the very problems we are trying to solve.

Get Them Gators!

If you want to create a working environment that is dominated by trust, fairness and cooperation where everyone has aligned incentives, you've got to *get them gators out of the equation.*

Slicing Pie is the solution—the *total* solution. *Slicing Pie* is a formula for implementing a dynamic equity split. There are two primary components of *Slicing Pie:*

1. The *Allocation* Framework that tells us how much each person should get; and,
2. The *Recovery* Framework, which tells us what to do when someone leaves the company.

As mentioned above, the model is dynamic, meaning that it changes over time to keep it fair. This part sometimes makes people nervous, but bear with me, as it will all make sense. Research has shown that companies that use dynamic models fare better than those that use fixed splits (as mentioned by Noam Wasserman in the Foreword). Some people think that fixed splits provide more certainty to participants. The only real certainty you will have is that you will eventually get thrown back into the gator pit!

Calculating Bets

Think back to the Blackjack analogy. In order to apply the *Slicing Pie* model, you have to know how to determine fair market value so you can calculate each person's bet. This is *much* easier to do than predicting the future!

For example, let's say you are an experienced programmer with many successful tech projects under your belt. Your time has a higher value than a young whipper-snapper right out of college with no concrete experience doing anything. Each of you could command a salary on the open market that is commensurate with your skills and experience.

Your respective fair market-rate salaries would account for expected contributions to a firm's productivity and would accommodate differences in skills, education and experience. All things being equal, your ability to add value to a company would be higher so you could command a higher salary. What an experienced programmer can do in a couple of hours might take the recent grad weeks or months.

If the company *pays* you your full market rate you are not putting anything at risk and, therefore, deserve no equity. If the company pays you *less* than your market rate, then you deserve equity *in proportion* to the amount that you're not getting paid. The same goes for the recent grad.

Adjustments

There are two primary types of contributions a person can contribute to a startup: cash and non-cash. Cash contributions consume a person's cash, while non-cash contributions do not. For example, time is a non-cash contribution and an unreimbursed expense is a cash contribution.

In most cases, it is much harder to *save* money than it is to *earn* money. A person who is earning $100,000 a year would be hard-pressed to save that amount in a year. Even if they could save *all* their money, they would be saving after-tax dollars, so a $100,000 annual salary would not mean $100,000 in the bank. The employer would pay employment tax and the employee would pay income tax. Lastly, when people actually buy stuff they have to pay sales tax or VAT tax or other taxes, which further reduce the buying power of money. Therefore, the person who contributes cash to a company is putting *more* at risk than the person who contributes time or other non-cash contributions.

Slicing Pie accounts for this difference by applying cash and non-cash multipliers (aka normalizers). The multipliers are explained, in detail, later in this book. For now, just think of this as an "adjusted" fair market value.

Everything Has a Fair Market Value

Later on this this book I'll provide detailed descriptions of how to calculate a fair market value for all kinds of possible contributions to a startup company including time, money, ideas, relationships, equipment, supplies and other important resources. Each calculation takes into account opportunity costs and the needs of the company.

Determining fair market value is usually pretty straightforward, but sometimes it's a little nuanced. For instance, the fair market value of a delivery truck has a lot to do with whether the truck was purchased for the company or if it has been sitting around in someone's backyard without being used for several years. In the former case, the fair market value is basically cash spent. In the latter case it has more to do with resale value.

The Slicing Pie Formula

If we substitute the adjusted fair market value or FMV (which is easy to calculate) for future value (which is impossible to calculate) we have a perfect substitute for our calculation. This:

$$\text{Your Share \%} = \frac{\text{The Value of Your Contribution}}{\text{The Total Value}}$$

Becomes:

$$\text{Your Share \%} = \frac{\text{The \textit{Adjusted FMV} of Your Contribution}}{\text{The Total \textit{Adjusted FMV}}}$$

In this book, the *Slicing Pie Handbook*, and on *SlicingPie.com*, I use the term "slices". A slice is a *fictional* unit used to represent the adjusted fair market value of an at-risk contribution. A slice does not represent equity shares, nor does it have any actual value; it just helps us to calculate the right percentages. The *Slicing Pie* formula is:

$$\text{Your Share \%} = \frac{\text{Your Slices}}{\text{All Slices}}$$

Slicing Pie in Action

Let's take a simple example of a fictional company where people contribute money, time, ideas, relationships and other resources. For purposes of simplicity, we will assume that each contribution has been converted to slices (S). There are two partners, Norvin and Anson. In the first quarter they each invest 100 S (which could be any mix of money, time, ideas, etc.).

	Quarter 1	Quarter 2	Quarter 3	Quarter 4	Total	Split
Anson	100 S				100 S	50%
Norvin	100 S				100 S	50%
					200 S	

It's logical that they would each own 50% of this business. And, because their contributions have been converted to slices, the contribution from Anson is "valued" the same as a contribution from Norvin, even though the company is probably worth nothing at this point. The next quarter Anson invests another 100 S and Norvin invests nothing. Maybe Norvin was busy with his day job that month. Here is what would happen if the split was fixed to 50/50:

	Quarter 1	Quarter 2	Quarter 3	Quarter 4	Total	Split
Anson	100 S	100 S			200 S	50%
Norvin	100 S	0 S			100 S	50%
					300 S	

In a *fixed* model Anson would have no incentive to invest the extra contribution because their split would stay 50/50. This isn't fair. Anson and Norvin would have to jump in the alligator pit and renegotiate their split. In a *dynamic* model the split would adjust based on the addition of extra contribution:

	Quarter 1	Quarter 2	Quarter 3	Quarter 4	Total	Split
Anson	100 S	100 S			200 S	67%
Norvin	100 S	0 S			100 S	33%
					300 S	

This is fair and both guys are happy knowing that they each have what they should. One might argue that earlier contribution is riskier, but measuring risk in a startup is as impossible as measuring future value.

What if, during the second quarter, the company's main client decides to cancel their contract? This would probably mean that the next round of contribution is actually *riskier* than earlier contributions. Considering this, Anson is more cautious, but Norvin is not:

	Quarter 1	Quarter 2	Quarter 3	Quarter 4	Total	Split
Anson	100 S	100 S	0 S		200 S	40%
Norvin	100 S	0 S	200 S		300 S	60%
					500 S	

In a dynamic model, each participant still has the right share. The ultimate value of the company is still unknown. All that *is* known is how much each person contributed *relative* to the other person. Anson has a smaller share, but he is comfortable with it because without Norvin's contribution the company may have failed. The following quarter neither one contributes anything because the company sells for $1,000,000.

	Quarter 1	Quarter 2	Quarter 3	Quarter 4	Total	Split
Anson	100 S	100 S	0 S	0 S	200 S	40%
Norvin	100 S	0 S	200 S	0 S	300 S	60%
					500 S	

Anson gets $400,000 and Norvin gets $600,000. This is *exactly* what they each should have had. Neither of them could have predicted that their company would sell for $1,000,000 in less than a year, but they each invested what was needed to move the company forward. The model was always in balance.

In most cases, people attempt to negotiate, in advance, how much money, time, supplies, etc., they will need. Next, they try to determine what the ultimate proceeds will be. Then they determine a fixed split. It's a nightmare. Without the dynamic feature, they will be thrown into the alligator pit, forced to renegotiate with gnashing teeth and swinging tails. *Nobody* wants to jump into an alligator pit.

In the *Slicing Pie* model, whether they are investing cash, time or other resources they can rest assured that at any given time they will always have exactly what they deserve relative to every other person, who will also have exactly what they deserve.

Saying Buh-Bye

One of the most disruptive events in an early-stage startup company is the departure of team members. These are often emotionally-charged times and the company winds up losing important talent that it might have to replace. It is at these times that equity splits become an issue and the alligators will rear their ugly heads.

The *Slicing Pie* model is designed to seamlessly handle these situations when it comes to what is fair for both the employee and the company.

There are four different situations under which a person can leave a company:

1. Termination for cause
2. Termination *without* cause
3. Resignation for good reason
4. Resignation for *no* good reason

In some cases, such as termination for cause, the company is left in the lurch and must scramble to replace the employee and make up for lost time. In cases like this, the employee bears the cost of departure, which provides a *disincentive* to slack off on the job. In other cases, such as resignation for good reason, the employee acted in good faith but the company made decisions that impacted their employment. In these cases, the company bears the cost of departure, which provides a *disincentive* to the management team for making decisions that adversely affect employees. Detailed descriptions of these circumstances are outlined later in this book and in *Slicing Pie*.

When someone leaves the company, the model will easily readjust to accommodate the change so that you, the participant, and the others will always have the fair amount.

Let's say, in our example above, that instead of selling in the second quarter, Norvin decided to bail out because he found a high-paying job somewhere else. This is resignation for no good reason. It may be a good reason to Norvin, but it's not a good reason for the company. In the *Slicing Pie* model Norvin bears the brunt of the cost and he would *lose* the equity he earned for any intangible contributions like time. (Tangible contributions like money and equipment are treated a little differently to mitigate the potential for fraud.)

For simplicity's sake, we'll pretend that Norvin *only* contributed time to the business. When he leaves he will lose his equity. *Ouch*! This isn't great for Norvin, but leaving means the company must scramble to replace him and this causes a great deal of pain for the company. If he wants to keep his share he should see the project through to the end. After he leaves, Anson owns 100% of the company, but has no partner.

	Quarter 1	Quarter 2	Quarter 3	Quarter 4	Total	Split
Anson	100 S	100 S			200 S	100%
Norvin						
					200 S	

Luckily, Anson is able to find Merrily, who can replace some of the skills that Norvin had. The *Slicing Pie* model easily accommodates her effort. Her contributions are converted to slices and the project moves forward.

	Quarter 1	Quarter 2	Quarter 3	Quarter 4	Total	Split
Anson	100 S	100 S	0 S		200 S	67%
Norvin						0%
Merrily			100 S		100 S	33%
					300 S	

It might take a little while longer for that $1,000,000 sale to happen, but they still have a chance. You might think it's weird to simply obliterate Novin's time, but it's actually quite logical. The calculations are not reflections of actual value; they are simply ways of determining the right split and aligning incentives. The company's *actual* value is still virtually nothing.

Let's say that Anson decides that the company should move to be closer to their largest client, who is 500 miles away. Merrily doesn't want to uproot her family and move and decides to resign. This is resignation with *good* reason. Anson's decision to move the company puts Merrily in a bad situation through no fault of her own. In this case, the company must bear the cost of this departure. Merrily is allowed to keep her slices in the company.

When Anson gets to the new location, he hires Anne to do the job that Merrily was doing.

	Quarter 1	Quarter 2	Quarter 3	Quarter 4	Total	Split
Anson	100 S	100 S	0 S	100 S	300 S	60%
Norvin						0%
Merrily			100 S		100 S	20%
Anne				100 S	100 S	20%
					500 S	

Once again, the dynamic model adjusts to keep everything fair. Relative to the others, everyone has what they deserve. Merrily still has a piece of the company because it wouldn't have been fair to take it back. Anne understands that Anson treated Merrily with fairness and is confident in working with him because she knows that she will be treated fairly too. Everybody is happy. Even Norvin is happy in his new job knowing that it was his choice to leave the company and that he doesn't deserve a slice of its success because he left them hanging when they needed him.

Conclusion

The point of this chapter was to pique your interest in *Slicing Pie* and dynamic equity splits in general by acclimating you to the basics of how they work and why they are important. I hope that you will see the value in the model and how it perfectly aligns incentives. Instead of wrestling alligators you can concentrate your attention on building a company with people who want to treat you fairly.

The rest of this book covers, in glorious detail, *exactly* how the model works. I'm going to repeat and go into more depth on the topics above to fully immerse you in the fairest equity split model ever conceived and how to implement it in *any* bootstrapped startup company on the planet.

Chapter Two:

Fix & Fight

The *Slicing Pie* model, described above and as
outlined in my original book on this topic, *Slicing
Pie: Funding Your Company Without Funds*, is a
structure for dividing up equity, or profit sharing,
in a startup company among early participants,
including founders, investors, employees, advisors,
partners or anyone else that provides contributions
for which the company cannot pay cash. If you
apply the model as outlined in this book, you will
enjoy a *perfectly fair* equity split no matter what.

The Traditional Model (Fix & Fight)

Most people, even super-smart people with great
experience and good intentions, struggle to create a
fair equity split because most of the conventional
wisdom around equity splitting makes it *impossible*
to achieve a fair split.

There are lots of reasons traditional models
cause problems, but the main problem is that most
people use *fixed* equity splits based largely on

future value creation. A fixed split means that chunks of equity are doled out to participants in pre-set amounts in *anticipation* of them creating value for the firm. Startup founders are nothing if not optimistic, but *accurately predicting the future* is a skill that eludes most mortals. Couple that with the *impossible* task of measuring value-add and you have a recipe for failure.

Of course, when things don't go *perfectly* according to plan, the team will have to go back to the drawing table, *renegotiate* the split and argue about value creation. The new split will rely on their *new* prediction of the future which, like the old one, will also be wrong.

This goes on and on throughout the early days of the company. Each round of painful renegotiations embitters the participants and pits them against one another as they fight about who is adding more value and what each person deserves.

Each round of battles often includes increased investment in legal agreements that include time-based vesting schedules and different classes of stock and option programs and hold-backs and all sorts of other things that simply apply a Band-Aid to the underlying problem, which is that fixed splits based on predictions about the future don't work. They only lead to fights.

Sometimes people will rely on "industry standards" about who should get what. Rules of thumb are everywhere, but the problem of the fixed split remains: unless everything goes according to plan, the split won't be right and another fight will ensue.

Every day, all over the world, well-meaning entrepreneurs enter into equity deals that backfire in ways that could easily destroy their dreams. Consider these scenarios:

> Frank, a marketing guy, starts a company. He hires Tom, a developer, and gives him 50% of the equity (Fix). Tom wants to hire some additional development help and wants to give the new guy 10%. Does the 10% come from Tom's share, Frank's, or both? (Fight.) *Slicing Pie* will allow them to sort this out.

> Jill, a developer, has an idea for a sports app. Joe, a marketing guy, *loves* the idea and agrees to sell it to his great contacts when it's ready. They split the equity 60% for Jill and 40% for Joe (Fix). Jill quits her job and works full time for a year to get the app ready for sale. Joe has moved onto other things and won't sell the app, but still wants to keep his 40% because he invested $5,000 (Fight). *Slicing Pie* won't allow Joe to do this, but will still treat him fairly.

> Len hires Miles and gives him 25% of the equity with a one-year vesting schedule (Fix). Miles works hard, does his job and

meets his goals. Len fires Miles for no reason a week before his first vesting date (Fight). *Slicing Pie* will not allow Len to take advantage of Miles.

Cindy hires Ron to build an app for her in exchange for 35% of the equity (Fix). She works hard to develop the market while Ron works part time to build the app. She pays Ron $40,000 over a six-month period— all her money. Ron finishes the app but decides he wants more money and more equity before turning it over to Cindy (Fight). *Slicing Pie* will not allow Ron to hold Cindy's software hostage.

John and Milton start a company and split the equity 50/50 (Fix). Within the first year, they have great success and become profitable. Milton gets killed in an accident and his wife, Molly, inherits his 50%. Now John has to do all the work himself. Does he have to give her 50% of all his profits? (Fight.) *Slicing Pie* will provide a moral solution that Molly will understand.

You and I go into business and split the equity 50/50 (Fix). You do all the work, but I own half the company... now what? (Fight.) *Slicing Pie* will give you recourse if I turn out to be a deadbeat!

Because all of these well-meaning founders used traditional Fix & Fight equity deals, they *all* face potentially insurmountable conflicts that could easily lead to the demise of the business.

Slicing Pie is the solution that all these founders need. It is the only equity model that will work. I believe *every founder on the planet* should use *Slicing Pie*. By the time you finish reading this book, I'm pretty sure you will agree!

Friends don't let friends Fix & Fight!

Chapter Three:

The Slicing Pie Principle

The *Slicing Pie* model is a **universal, one-size-fits-all solution for bootstrapped startups**. I realize this is a **bold** statement, especially in a world where "it depends" is so common. However, I make this statement because I believe the model can apply *anywhere*. When I designed the model, it was my intent to make it universal.

The reason I think the *Slicing Pie* model is universal is because the basic principle behind *Slicing Pie* is profoundly simple and unambiguous. The ***Slicing Pie* Principle** is:

Your % share of the reward
=
Your % share of what's at risk

The *reward* I'm talking about is financial and comes in the form of profits/dividends or the proceeds of a sale. What's *at risk* are contributions of time, money, ideas, relationships or anything else participants invest in a startup and don't get paid. *Everyone deserves a slice of the rewards that properly reflects their slice of what's put at risk to achieve those rewards.*

Some people believe their share of the reward should be *greater* than their share of what's at risk. But most people don't want to work with someone who is willing to benefit at the expense of others.

Hardly anyone believes their share of the rewards should be *less* than their share of what's at risk. When someone realizes they are being taken advantage of, they become angry, resentful and unmotivated to perform.

Most people know that they deserve what they deserve, no more and no less. I hope you're one of these people.

The ideal startup team consists of people who want to work together to generate rewards and take only what they deserve. *Slicing Pie is about doing right by those who help your company succeed.*

At-Risk Contributions Before Breakeven

To dig down a little deeper, consider a typical breakeven graph like the one below.

The plotted line represents income which is revenue – expenses. In the beginning, income is negative. Participants are either spending their own money or otherwise *not* getting paid for their contribution. *After* the breakeven point, revenue *exceeds* expenses. At this point, participants are getting reimbursed for expenses (or the company is paying the bills) and they are being compensated for their efforts. In other words, *after breakeven, an individual's new contributions are no longer at-risk*, because they are getting paid.

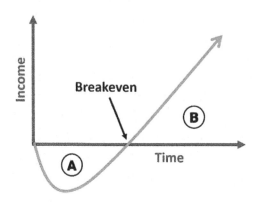

What's *really* important to note is that at the point of breakeven, area A, representing the at-risk contributions, is *quantifiable* and *knowable*. However, the future income generated by the company, area B, is *unknowable*.

Slicing Pie is used *before* breakeven. Equity is based on what people put at-risk. *After* breakeven everyone is getting paid, so equity is no longer about what's at-risk.

After breakeven or in established companies, equity is sometimes part of a bonus or retention strategy.

The Slicing Pie Formula

If you buy into the basic *Slicing Pie* principle, then the formula that *Slicing Pie* uses to allocate equity should be easy to understand:

$$\text{Your Share (\%)} = \frac{\textbf{What You Put At Risk}}{\textbf{Everything That's At Risk}}$$

What's *at risk* in the *Slicing Pie* model, as I will explain in much detail below, is a function of the **fair market value** of a contribution (like time, money, ideas, etc.) and a **risk multiplier** that *normalizes* cash and non-cash contributions and imposes consequences on the at-fault party in the event of a person's separation from the company.

It's Not Complicated

Slicing Pie is not complex. It is simple and obvious. To apply the model, however, you will have to keep track of what each person puts at risk.

The reason I've written *entire books* on this topic is not because the model is complicated, but because I want to help everyone figure out how to determine and track the fair market value of their contributions and what to do when someone leaves.

Keeping track of contributions requires a little structure and discipline. The good news is that if you are part of a team that values structure and discipline you're probably much more likely to succeed.

Slicing Pie is for Bootstrappers

The *Slicing Pie* model is best suited for startup companies that are bootstrapped during the early stages of development.

Startups use the model until sufficient cash is available to *pay* participants for their contributions. This is usually when the company starts generating revenue or when the founders raise Series A investment.

When everybody is getting paid for their contributions (after breakeven), they will no longer be putting their contributions at risk. At this point the model will essentially "freeze," and, subsequently, it will tell the managers how to divide up profits, if and when they are dispersed. Or, it will tell managers how to divide up the proceeds of a sale. The profits a company generates or the proceeds from a sale are the *rewards* of a startup. Remember, a person's % share of the rewards should equal their % share of what's put at risk.

Slicing Pie is Better Than Traditional Fixed Splits

The *Slicing Pie* model mitigates the potential for fights that often arise from a traditional Fix & Fight model. In a fixed-split model, equity is allocated at the outset of the venture, often in equal amounts, among founders (e.g., "50/50" or "25/25/25/25" or "51/49). It is not uncommon for such agreements to be poorly documented "handshake" agreements between overly optimistic founders.

The basis for fixed split allocations are industry trends, *guesses* about future value, advice from well-meaning advisors or negotiation skills. Even *if* a fair allocation could be achieved using a fixed model, the allocation would cease to be fair the moment something changes or unanticipated events occur. All startups go through change.

Disagreements with fixed-split allocations often arise when members of the team are added or subtracted, or the work product of individual participants differs from what the team originally anticipated. At the core of these complaints is a general feeling of unfairness, mistrust, and greed as participants, lacking an objective measure of fairness, attempt to get the highest possible share for themselves, even if it's at the expense of other participants. Such disputes can lead to unnecessary legal expenses, unpopular pay-offs or buyouts of various employees, and a deterioration of working relationships that may ultimately lead to the demise of the company. Most corporate and startup attorneys are all too familiar with such disputes. There is plenty of work for lawyers in the Fix & Fight model.

At first glance, fixed splits will *appear easier* to implement than the *Slicing Pie* model. The hard part about fixed splits isn't implementing them; it's *unwinding* them when you realize you've made a mistake. *Fixing* a fixed split model can be extremely complex legally, financially and emotionally. You're much better implementing the *Slicing Pie* model and spending the rest of your efforts on building your business instead of fighting with team members.

Slicing Pie reflects reality, the Fix & Fight model is all make-believe.

Allocation and Recovery

The *Slicing Pie* model provides a means to avoid such disagreements by laying out a universal framework for both the *allocation* of equity or profit sharing in the company and the *recovery* of outstanding slices in the event of an individual's separation from the company.

The **allocation framework** tells you how to give slices to individuals as they make contributions to the company. It is a dynamic model, meaning that it changes over time. This means that at any given time *all* participants will have *exactly* what they should have, regardless of changes in the strategy or the team. With fixed allocations, it is *impossible* to have a fair split—each person always has too much or too little.

The **recovery framework** tells you what to do when someone leaves the company. In some cases, the company will be able to recover outstanding slices for no or low cost; in other cases, the person leaving will be entitled to keep their share or sell it back at a fair premium. It depends on the nature of the separation. The recovery framework ensures that each participant understands the consequences of their decisions as they relate to ongoing participation in the firm.

An absentee owner is someone who owns equity or profit sharing in your company but is no longer actively involved. It is best to avoid this situation if possible. The recovery framework provides a means for buying out ex-employees if and when appropriate.

A Moral Agreement

Although the *Slicing Pie* model can be part of a legal contract (you will find contract templates at SlicingPie.com), at the core of the model is a *moral* agreement. It's about doing right by the people who help you succeed. When implemented as outlined herein, it provides a structure for fair play, favors no one person over another, and ensures that everyone receives what they deserve.

In my experience, most people *want* to treat others fairly, but they may not know exactly how given the limitations of conventional wisdom and practice. The *Slicing Pie* model is the how. It will help the people who mean well to *do* well.

Of course, greed can be a powerful force that sometimes causes people to act in unscrupulous ways. Greed is when a person has a strong desire to have more than they deserve. A person may act within the law to capture value for themselves at the expense of others, but just because something is *legal* doesn't mean it's *fair*.

Some people are so overcome by greed that fairness doesn't seem to matter at all. Perhaps you will be able to avoid these people in your career as an entrepreneur. It's not always easy; but even if you find yourself in an uncomfortable situation, the *Slicing Pie* model can help. Applying the model will tell you the extent to which you are being taken advantage of so you can make better decisions about what to do next.

A person's willingness to apply the *Slicing Pie* model could be an indicator of their intent to be fair. If I find someone who *doesn't* want to use this model, I don't join their startup, nor do I ask them to join mine. Don't get me wrong; I'm not saying this model is an *absolute* measure of a person's character, and I realize that a person's unwillingness to collaborate using this model doesn't mean they are a greedy or immoral person. But why add the risk? Startups are already risky.

Startup Risk

In finance, risk & return go hand-in-hand. When an individual, or a team of individuals, embarks upon a new venture, they are accepting risk and putting their contributions at risk. The risk they are accepting is the risk that they will never get paid for their contributions of time, money, ideas, relationships and anything else consumed by the company in the process of realizing its vision.

Anyone who accepts this risk deserves a slice of the pie that reflects this risk *relative* to other participants who also accepted risk.

If a person takes *no* risk, he doesn't deserve any return. If a person takes *100%* of the risk, he deserves 100% of the return. If two or more people *share* in the risk, they each deserve a portion of the return that properly reflects that risk relative to the other person. If one person puts $100 at risk and another person puts $1,000 at risk, the person who put in $1,000 has taken more risk *relative* to the person who put in $100. If the other person also put in $1,000, then both people risked the same relative to one another.

If one person took 90% of the risk and the other took 10%, it wouldn't be fair to split the return 50/50. Splitting the return 90/10 is more appropriate. If the two people accepted the same level of risk, it would be appropriate to provide the same return.

Betting On a Startup

Think back to the Blackjack analogy from the introduction. Like in Blackjack, when someone contributes to a startup company they are, in effect, placing a *bet* on the future outcome of the startup. The good news is that, unlike the future, the amount of risk each participant is accepting when they make a contribution is *very specific* and *measurable. It is* equal *to the amount that they otherwise get paid by someone else for the same contribution.* This amount, also known as "fair market value," is easily observable in the marketplace.

In other words, when a person contributes to a startup they are *betting* the fair market value of that contribution on the future outcome of the startup.

The fair market value of a year of a person's time, for instance, is equal to their salary for a similar job at a company that had the means to pay. So, if you forego that salary to work for a startup (doing similar work), you are *betting* that amount of money. The opportunity cost of working for a startup is *equal* to the amount of money you would have earned elsewhere doing a *similar* job. Similarly, the fair market value of office space is *equal* to the amount of money the landlord can charge for that space. So, if the landlord allows you to use the office space at no cost, they are *betting* the amount of money they would have otherwise received from someone who had the money to pay.

People bet whatever they *contribute* to the startup effort. Every contribution is what it is. Nothing *magic* happens just because you make a contribution to a startup. The only difference is you're not getting paid the fair market rate. For instance, you may spend weeks working on a problem before you come up with a brilliant solution. The minute that you come up with the solution doesn't magically become more valuable than all the other minutes you spent on the job any more than the pencil you used to write down the idea doesn't become more valuable than any other pencil. But, even if it did become more valuable, it is *impossible* to measure the value it created.

Because fair market value is so easy to observe, it can be used as an important component for the calculation of ownership or other interest in the income generated by a startup company. Using easily observable values means we don't have to guess. Most of this book and the *Slicing Pie* book is about how to determine fair market value and apply the formula.

Multipliers/Normalizing

The only reason a rational person would be willing to join a startup and accept this risk is if they believe that their ultimate compensation will *far exceed* the amount they would otherwise get paid. Unfortunately, the chance of this happening is *very* low, and the risk of receiving nothing is *very* high. Indeed, startups are *extremely* risky.

Because startups are so risky, the other major component used in calculating ownership or other interest in a startup, besides fair market value, is a *multiplier* that will not only reward an individual for taking that risk, but also normalize cash and non-cash contributions. The multipliers also create consequences for the at-fault party in the event of a separation. *Multipliers are the secret ingredient that makes Slicing Pie work.*

A Slice of the Pie

The way an individual reaps the benefits of a company's financial return is through their individual entitlement to a slice of the Pie. In many cases, this would imply equity ownership in the company (and I promote the model as such), but it does not have to. As long as an individual receives distributions of cash in proportion to their slice of the Pie, they should be happy, regardless of the underlying ownership structure.

For instance, if I own 100% of the equity in a company, but you, as my partner, contribute (risk) 19% of the contributions necessary to make the company worth something, you are entitled to 19% of the Pie. So, when the company distributes profits, you should receive 19% of the money. Or, if the company sells, you should receive 19% of the proceeds. Beyond that, the underlying ownership isn't important as long as you receive the payout you deserve. This is called "profit sharing" and may be an acceptable option for your company. A profit-sharing program can include ways to easily buy-out individuals at a fair price.

Equity can imply decision-making control over the company, so issuing actual equity in the company may complicate the individual roles people play. Founders wishing to maintain decision-making control of their companies have some options depending on the legal structure of the company. I'll cover more on this later.

Your team can decide whether to issue actual equity shares or profit sharing in the company. Both scenarios will have legal and tax implications that I will address later on. There are some *Slicing Pie* lawyers on SlicingPie.com, who can help you figure this out.

Slices

A "slice" is a fictional unit of measure that reflects the adjusted at-risk contributions made by individual participants. Slices will allow you to calculate equity or profit sharing. This is not the same thing as a share, which is a legal unit of ownership.

NOTE: If you read *Slicing Pie* version 2.3 or earlier, you'll notice that I don't use the term "slice." In that book, I use the term "theoretical value." **Slices** and **Theoretical Values** are the same things.

The Pie Slicer Application

You may have noticed by now that *Slicing Pie* requires you and your team to keep track of the contributions made by different people including time and money.

You and your team can keep track in whatever level of granularity that you are comfortable with, but I recommend logging hours on a daily or weekly basis and organizing time and expenses based on projects.

Like many things in business, keeping track of time and money can be tedious. The **Pie Slicer** application is an online tool that is designed to make this process as painless as possible. You can find it at SlicingPie.com

Throughout this handbook, I will refer to the online Pie Slicer Application and how to use it to keep track of your equity split. More detail about getting started is in the Pie Slicer chapter. You do not *have* to use the online tools to be successful. As long as you keep track of what's going on in your company, you will be fine.

Pie Slicer

Boxes like this one will provide information about how to get the most from the Pie Slicer application. If you're not using the Pie Slicer, you can skip these boxes!

Summary

Slicing Pie is based on the basic principle that a person's % share of the reward should equal their % share of the at-risk contributions. This means that this simple dynamic formula will allow you to calculate a perfect split:

$$\text{Individual's Share (\%)} = \frac{\text{Individual's Slices}}{\text{Total Slices of all Participants}}$$

Today, the most common type of equity split is a "fixed" split. This means that chunks of equity are doled out to participants at the outset of a venture in *anticipation* of their future contributions.

Fixed splits are based on unobservable information like future value or are based on industry "standards" and negotiation skills. *All* fixed splits become unfair the moment something changes, leading to disagreements among early participants that can escalate and possibly destroy a company.

The *Slicing Pie* model is a framework for the fair allocation and recovery of equity or profit sharing based on the fair market value. The fair market value of a contribution is the amount of money that the contributor would have been paid by someone else for the same contribution in a given market. This, combined with a risk multiplier/normalizer, gives us everything we need to calculate a perfectly fair split among all participants in a startup.

At the heart of the *Slicing Pie* model is a moral contract. It is about doing right by those who help you succeed.

Chapter Four:

Allocation Framework

The allocation framework applies the *Slicing Pie* Formula to determine a person's share of the at-risk contributions (aka "bets"). To break down the steps, I'll cover a basic set of calculations. These define the number of slices added to the Pie in exchange for various contributions, and are based on the fair market value of the contribution and a multiplier to normalize cash and non-cash inputs.

Non-cash contributions include time, ideas, relationships (that turn into customers, suppliers, employees or investors), pre-owned equipment or supplies, and some resources such as office space. Cash contributions consist primarily of unreimbursed expenses and, of course, cash.

Using the calculations from the allocation framework, an individual's contributions are *converted to slices* and their portion of the company is calculated on a *rolling* basis using the following formula at any given time:

$$\text{Individual's Share (\%)} \quad = \quad \frac{\text{Individual's Slices}}{\text{Total Slices of all Participants}}$$

The formula *ensures* that equity or profit sharing allocation remains fair, in spite of changes the firm might encounter. As time goes by, work is done, people come and go, sales are made, and business is conducted. The number of slices in the model is therefore always changing because each day, more bets are placed.

You may be uncomfortable with the dynamic nature of the model at first. Once you get your head around how this works however, you will see the importance of the dynamic model and its ability to ensure fairness. I *promise* that if you use this model, you will *always* have what you deserve. You may not have what you *desire*, but you will certainly have what you *deserve*.

The dynamic model takes into account the inherent volatility of a startup environment, whereas a fixed split makes the false assumption that the future can be known or accurately predicted or that everyone always does exactly what they say they are going to do. Under *all* circumstances, a dynamic model is going to be fairer than a fixed model.

Certainty

It's not uncommon for people unfamiliar with *Slicing Pie* to worry that it may provide less certainty than a fixed model. This misconception stems from the false belief that a fixed split can accurately reflect the future. It can't. The only real certainty you get from a fixed split is the certainty that you will have to renegotiate your split when something doesn't go as planned!

Renegotiating an equity split is a painful experience that rarely leaves people feeling good. It puts startup participants at odds and can easily lead to the demise of the business.

If your team wants to be *certain* about this horrible fate, use a Fix & Fight split. If they want to be *certain* about being treated fairly, use *Slicing Pie*.

Calculations

To convert an individual contribution into slices, simply multiply the fair market value of the contribution (less cash payments) by the cash or non-cash multiplier. You subtract cash payments, if any, because cash payments reduce the amount of risk taken. If the company pays 100% of the fair market value it shouldn't have to provide equity at all because the individual isn't putting any salary at-risk.

Although it's possible for team members to disagree on fair market value, I will outline best practices below. In spite of potential difficulties, fair market value is much less subjective than a typical startup valuation, which is based on future events.

Multipliers/Normalizers

Multipliers/normalizers assign a risk premium for the contributions, adjust for the difference between cash and non-cash contributions and help determine the fair buyout price if and when someone separates from the company. The multipliers impose important consequences for the at-fault party. Think of the multipliers as a built-in *retention* tool for companies and a built-in *severance* program for employees. (More on this when I cover the Recovery Framework).

 **Pie Slicer**

Click **Pie Settings** to see what you can tweak about your own Pie. Make sure that all participants know what you edit. On the print version of this handbook, you can record the values in the spaces provided on the page right after the dedication page.

I recommend a non-cash multiplier of two (2x) and a cash multiplier of four (4x). These numbers are set based on my personal experience with the model and they are important. *Resist the urge to change them!* The multipliers make the model work. Without them, you will be less successful in achieving a fair split. One of the most common questions I get about *Slicing Pie* is why cash is weighted twice as much as non-cash. There are some important reasons for this:

Scarcity

Cash is given a higher premium because it's much harder to *save* money than it is to *earn* money. The multipliers recognize the difference in scarcity between cash and non-cash contributions. Most (not all) people have more time than money. The higher multiplier provides incentives to people to contribute cash. After all, cash is king!

Taxes

You may not have noticed that non-cash calculations use *pre-tax* dollars and cash calculations use *post-tax* dollars.

For example, if you earn $100 in one hour you would *not* be able to buy something that costs $100 after working for one hour. Before the company pays you, they will have to deduct payroll taxes. Next, you will pay income tax on what's leftover. Then, when you go and buy the $100 thing, you will pay sales tax or VAT tax or whatever other taxes your country likes. So, to buy a $100 thing, you'll have to work *more* than an hour, maybe even two hours. The higher cash multiplier helps compensate for this difference.

Alignment with Investors

Investors want to make sure that managers make smart decisions with their money. A higher multiplier for cash means that startup managers will think twice before spending money knowing that cash is more "expensive" than non-cash when it comes to slices. This not only helps ensure they are being conservative with cash, but also provides an incentive to generate revenue faster. This is what investors want. The higher cash multiplier aligns the interests of the management team and the investors.

Floating Multipliers

Sometimes people think that the multipliers should change, or "float" over time to reflect the possibility that risk goes down over time. Early contributions, they argue, are riskier than later contributions, so the risk multiplier should go down over time.

I completely understand the logic, but in practice startups are far too volatile to ascertain a definitive level of risk. The risk may *appear* to go down as the company gains traction and generates revenue, but if the company loses a major customer, the risk may go up. Similarly, if a company grows so fast that they can't provide a meaningful level of service, risk could go up.

Startups have so many ups and downs that trying to predict risk at any given time is futile. In the *Slicing Pie* model, you have to measure what you can. Because of this, please keep the multipliers constant. They are a key part of why the *Slicing Pie* model works so well for so many companies. If you're still not convinced, you are free to change the multipliers or eliminate them completely. Just don't be surprised when you run into problems!

 Pie Slicer

Although I don't recommend changing the multipliers, some people do it anyway. Because of this, you can change the multipliers in the Pie Slicer. For best results, make sure your cash multiplier is more than your non-cash multiplier and that your non-cash multiplier is higher than one.

To change the multipliers, go to **Settings → Pie Settings** and look for the Non-Cash and Cash Multiplier Settings.

Any changes you make to any settings will impact future contributions only; it will not recalculate the existing Pie.

Summary

A "slice" is a fictional unit of measure that allows entrepreneurs to allocate a percentage of the pie based on observable values instead of guesses about the future. Slices reflect what someone *would get paid* for the same contribution to another company that could pay and a multiplier/normalizer that reflects the high risk of never getting paid at all. A company uses slices when it can't pay cash.

There are two steps to allocate equity, or profit sharing, in your business. First, convert contributions to slices:

Slices = Fair Market Value x Multiplier (Cash or Non-Cash)

Because cash is more difficult to come by than other types of contributions, I recommend a cash multiplier of four (4x) and a non-cash multiplier of two (2x).

Next, apply this formula which will tell you an individual's contribution relative to other contributors.

$$\text{Individual's Share (\%)} = \frac{\text{Individual's Slices}}{\text{Total Slices of all Participants}}$$

The model is dynamic, so it adjusts over time to make sure that at any given time, everyone always has what they deserve no matter what changes.

There's really not much to it. The formula simply calculates one person's risk relative to the others. Most of this book is about converting to slices using fair market value.

Chapter Five:

Cash Contributions

A cash contribution is a contribution that consumes an individual participant's actual cash, usually in the form of an unreimbursed expense or cash expenditure from the company account. A cash contribution can also be tangible property with cash value like equipment or supplies. The formula to determine slices is as follows:

Slices = Fair Market Value x Cash Multiplier

If you're dealing with actual cash, then the fair market value is equal to the amount of cash *spent*. If the cash isn't spent, it's not at risk. It's just sitting in the bank. Slices get allocated when the cash gets spent.

The Well

It is usually not a good idea to make a habit of paying expenses from a personal account if it can be avoided. Founders, friends, family, and small angel investors can contribute cash to a company savings account. I call this account "the Well."

The Well is a pool of funds from which managers can make payments. They can use the money for whatever they need to, subject to the restrictions of the investor, if any. You can pay salaries or rent, for instance, with money you draw from the Well.

Money in the Well does not convert to slices at the time of deposit. Instead, slices are created when the company spends the money. Remember, slices represent at-risk contributions in a startup. If cash is sitting in a savings account, it's not really at risk because managers could simply return the money to the investor. It is at risk only when it gets spent or otherwise tied up. For instance, your landlord may require a security deposit. Money in the landlord's account *is* at risk.

When money is drawn from the Well and put into a company checking account to pay bills, it converts to slices for each Well participant in proportion to their current ownership of the Well money. Because it converts to slices at the higher cash multiplier, managers are always mindful not to overspend. This is a good thing because it helps them focus and be smart with money. This, like all aspects of the model, aligns the interest of the investors and employees.

❋ Pie Slicer

Add money to the Well by clicking **Add Funds to Well** in the top left of the Pie Slicer.

If one team member was responsible for securing the cash investment, they might be entitled to a Finder's Fee. More on this later...

For example, Julie and Chuck want to help Anne start a cinnamon roll shop, and they each put $10,000 into a company savings account for a total Well of $20,000. Anne needs $1,000 to cover the current month's expenses, so she transfers the money to the company checking account. Because both Julie and Chuck have 50% ownership of the cash in the Well, $500 is attributed to each of them, and they each receive 2,000 slices of Pie (cash times four). The following month, Anne draws an additional $4,000 from the Well. Julie and Chuck each receive 8,000 slices. Anne is careful only to draw what she needs, so she doesn't have to give up too many slices. Julie and Chuck know that she has an incentive to be smart with their money.

Now the Well has $15,000 left. Suzanne is an investor who gives her another $15,000, so now the Well is $30,000. Suzanne owns 50% and Julie and Chuck each own 25%.

Anne buys an oven that costs $10,000. $5,000 is attributed to Suzanne, so she receives 20,000 slices. Julie and Chuck each receive 10,000 slices for their $2,500 contribution or 25% of the total.

🥧 Pie Slicer

Draw money from the Well by clicking **Draw Funds from Well** in the top left of the Pie Slicer.

The Well will automatically allocate the slices to team members in proportion to their ownership of the money in the Well at the time it is drawn.

If the Well balance reaches zero, all slices will have been allocated for that "round."

The Well helps managers keep money on hand, but protects the Pie from being "swamped" by too much cash. Cash converts to slices only when the company spends it.

Slicing Pie attorneys can provide a simple Well agreement for people who contribute to the Well. Visit SlicingPie.com and look for the "Resources" or "A La Mode" tab for more information.

The Well agreement is essentially a loan agreement for money that goes into the company savings account where it will stay until it is used by the managers. When withdrawals are made from the savings account the amount of the withdrawal is treated as a payment towards the balance on the loan. At the same time, the money converts to slices in the Pie.

Unless required by law, there typically isn't any interest on the Well agreement. When people put money into the Well, their intent isn't to make loans with loan interest. If they are, they should ask for a traditional loan. Some investors are more comfortable with loans than equity.

The Well is best for active participants in the company. For arms-length investors, a traditional convertible note or convertible equity agreement is easier, and it represents the fair market for small investments. The SAFE (Simple Agreement for Future Equity) from YCombinator is a good option.

Unreimbursed Expenses

The most common cash contribution from employees is an unreimbursed expense. This is money spent on just about anything for the firm that does not get reimbursed from the company account (Well).

Examples:

- Norvin pays $2,500 for the cost of an attorney to write a customer contract and does *not* get reimbursed from the company account. Norvin would receive 10,000 slices.
- Anson pays $250 for a train ticket to take a company trip to Amsterdam and does not get reimbursed from the company account. Anson would receive 1,000 slices.
- Merrily uses her credit card to buy a client a $40 dinner and only gets reimbursed $10 from the company account. Merrily would receive 120 slices (($40-$10) x 4).
- Anne pays $30 a month to take the train to the offices of her startup company and does

not get reimbursed. Anne *would not* receive any Pie.

Notice that, in the last example, Anne does *not* receive any Pie even though she incurred an expense that was business related and she did not get reimbursed. This is because her expense was a commuting expense and it is not customary to reimburse commuting expenses. Most employers—at least in the USA—don't reimburse expenses associated with getting to work, so the startup shouldn't give Pie. Similarly, if Anne buys lunch for herself, she can't ask for Pie either. Generally speaking, if it's not customary to cover an expense for employees in your country or local market, you don't have to provide Pie.

To be clear, when employees use their own money to pay for things on behalf of the company and do not get paid back, this is an unreimbursed expense. The money they use does not go into the Well because it's spent on a specific item. The Well is used to hold larger amounts of money for future expenses. Money in the Well could be used to reimburse employees, in which case the owners of the Well would receive slices, not the employee.

Employees and other contributors should keep track of expenses and save receipts so they can accurately report their expenses.

At first, it might feel strange to provide slices for small, seemingly insignificant expenses, but over time these things can add up. It's not fair to ask someone to cover business expenses. Unless employees get rewarded for their contribution, they will begin to resent their job and morale will suffer.

 **Pie Slicer**

Under each user, there is a pull-down menu that provides access to entry fields for various contributions.

Personal Car

When a person uses his personal car for business purposes, it is customary to provide reimbursement. In the United States and as of this writing, the Internal Revenue Service (IRS) sets a tax-deductible rate of around $0.54 per mile, so many employers pay this amount to employees who use their own car. This amount reflects both fuel costs and wear & tear on the car itself. In the *Slicing Pie* model, this presents a problem because the reimbursement represents both a cash (fuel) and a non-cash (wear & tear) contribution.

There are a couple of ways to handle this; either is fine as long as you let people know in advance and keep the calculation consistent for everyone. Calculations include:

1. Use the cash *or* non-cash multiplier for the whole amount.
2. Calculate the personal car reimbursement and *subtract* the out-of-pocket fuel cost. Apply the cash multiplier to the fuel cost and the non-cash multiplier to the rest. This

is the most accurate, but requires people to track their fuel expenses.

 **Pie Slicer**

You can set the Personal Car calculation method and rate in the Settings Menu. The Pie Slicer makes splitting the expense easy. If you are using a spreadsheet, applying the cash or non-cash multiplier to the whole amount will be easier.

Loans and Credit Cards

Sometimes, an individual uses personal credit to secure a loan on behalf of the company or puts expenses on their credit card. If the individual is making the payments on the loan, the money is treated as cash when the money is spent. If the loan is a lump sum for general purposes, it becomes part of the Well and slices are given when the money is drawn out. If the loan is used to buy something specific, the money is spent and converts immediately to slices.

However, if the loan is taken out in the individual's name, but is being paid back by the company instead of the individual, the individual *does not* receive any slices. Yes, the individual *is* taking risk for securing the loan with personal credit, but because they aren't *personally* making the payments, they don't receive any slices. At first this may seem unfair, but it's not.

If someone gives you money and expects *you* to make regular payments, they are giving you a loan. It does not matter where the money comes from; all that matters is that the nature of the transaction is a loan. The lender would be within their rights to ask for interest on the loan, but they do not deserve a slice of the Pie. If they *did* receive a slice of the Pie, the loan would, in effect, be double-counted in the Pie. The person providing the loan would be receiving Pie and the person paying or providing the cash to repay the loan would be receiving Pie. This just doesn't work.

Risk Tolerance

Slicing Pie does not take a person's risk tolerance into account when calculating slices. It only accounts for *actual* at-risk contributions. If someone has a low tolerance for risk, they may feel a high level of anxiety when contributing money to a startup. This doesn't change the fair market value of the money, however.

Someone with a high tolerance for risk may invest their life savings, but this doesn't change the fair market value of the money they actually invest.

A basic rule about investing is not to invest any more than you can afford to lose. If you can't tolerate the risk, don't contribute the cash!

So, loans and credit card expenses are treated as cash (4x) *if* the individual who provided the loan is making the payments. *If* the company is making the payments—with or without additional interest—no slices are granted.

When cash-money is spent on behalf of the company, and the individual who provided the cash is not paid back, the fair market value of the cash is equal to the cash spent.

Fair Market Value = Amount of Cash Spent

Supplies & Equipment

Many companies require supplies and equipment to get into business. A T-shirt company needs printing presses and dryers. A hamburger stand needs a grill and spatulas. A tech company needs computers. A zoo needs cages and at least a couple of nice llamas.

If these things are purchased for the company and the person who purchased them was not reimbursed from the company account, the fair market value would be the price they paid.

Slices = Price Paid x Cash Multiplier

However, in many cases, people may have equipment that they acquired some other way. Someone may keep llamas as pets, for example, and provide some for the start-up zoo. Or perhaps someone has an old truck that the startup can use for deliveries. Transferring ownership of a pre-owned asset into a company isn't the same as spending cash. It's a non-cash contribution. Therefore, it represents a different level of risk and slices are at the non-cash rate. If the supplies or equipment are *less than a year old*, the model uses the purchase price.

Slices = Price Paid x Non-Cash Multiplier

If the supplies or equipment are *more than a year old*, the model uses the resale price. You can find the current resale price fairly easily by looking on eBay.com, Craigslist, or industry classified listings for similar supplies or equipment.

Slices = Resale Price x Non-Cash Multiplier

It's important to note that when slices are received, the supplies and equipment become the property of the company. This means that if the person who contributed the equipment leaves the company, they can't take the stuff with them. However, as you'll see in the chapter on the Recovery Framework, the person may be entitled to some kind of payment.

Pie Slicer

The Supplies screen and the Equipment screen are the same in the Pie Slicer. Users will be asked the amount paid or the fair market value and the age of the contribution so it can apply the appropriate rule.

In many cases, personal laptops or cellphones used in building the company would *not* be treated as contributed equipment and people who own them would *not* receive slices. The company, therefore, would *not* own these items and departing employees can take them when they leave.

Similarly, small amounts of supplies brought from home may not warrant slices. Use your best judgment here; a person probably doesn't deserve slices for bringing a tape dispenser and some old pens to the office.

Cash contributions or tangible contributions will have special treatment in the event of separation, which I will cover in detail in the chapter about recovery.

Summary

A cash contribution is a contribution that consumes an individual's cash. Because cash is harder to come by than time (for most people) *and* we use after-tax values, it gets a higher multiplier than non-cash contributions.

Slices are allocated when the cash is *spent*, because *un*spent money is not at risk and slices represent risk.

The Well is a tool that can be used to hold unspent money until it is needed for expenses. When money is transferred out of the Well, the Well owners get slices in proportion to their ownership of the cash in the Well.

When an individual takes on personal debt for the company they receive slices when the money is spent as long as they are paying the payments on the loan. If the company is paying the payments then no slices are allocated.

Unreimbursed expenses or purchases of new equipment and supplies for the company are treated as cash contributions. When slices are provided, the company takes ownership of these assets.

Contributions of pre-owned equipment and supplies are treated as non-cash contributions and use the non-cash multiplier.

Chapter Six:

Non-Cash Contributions

A non-cash contribution is pretty much anything an individual contributes *without* an outlay of cash. Time is an example of a non-cash contribution. There are no direct expenses associated with the time I spend working on a startup. Similarly, there are no direct costs associated with introducing the company to a qualified prospect I might know.

Many startups can be built with mostly non-cash contributions — often referred to as "sweat equity." A tech startup, for instance, may be able to be created without spending a dime. In fact, the real beauty of the *Slicing Pie* Method is its ability to fairly account for non-cash contributions and use slices to reward the people who made them. Most companies, however, will require a mix of cash and non-cash contributions to be successful.

To convert non-cash contributions into slices, use the following calculation:

Slices = Fair Market Value of Contribution x 2

However, for this to work you need to have a way of determining the fair market value of the contributions. This is not difficult if you know how.

Magic ATM Card

One way to think about how to determine fair market value is to imagine you had a magic ATM card that would give you access to all the money you needed as long as you didn't waste it. If the card senses you are being frivolous, it will stop working, so you can't pay yourself a $10 million salary, for example.

Now, because of the card, you can simply pay for everything you need. You can pay employees, rent, utilities, sales commissions—everything! The non-frivolous amount you would pay is the fair market value.

So, if you are a smart shopper you can negotiate the right price for the things you need, but instead of paying, you'll simply add slices to the pie! This is the basic idea, and I'll provide more detail below.

Time

Most employed people do not receive equity as part of their compensation package and are perfectly happy as long as they feel they are being paid what they deserve. The "perfectly happy" price is the fair market value of their time as long as their work for the startup is similar to what they would do for someone else at a fair market rate.

For example, if a person is "perfectly happy" making $50,000 a year as a marketing executive, they should be willing to accept a similar amount for similar work at a startup (to be paid in Pie). However, if that person is leaving their job as a marketing executive to flip burgers at a burger startup, the fair market rate would be the rate at which the person would otherwise be paid to flip burgers at a similar establishment. Big companies, like McDonalds or In 'N' Out Burger, are likely to have a significant influence on the fair market rate for burger-flippers.

A *Slicing Pie* salary negotiation, therefore, is like any other salary negotiation. A manager should ask herself, "*If* I could pay cash for this person's services, how much would I pay?" A potential employee should ask himself, "*If* this company paid me and did not give me equity, how much would I be perfectly happy to accept?" If there is an overlap between these two numbers, a deal can be struck; if not, you can part ways as friends.

When the company eventually (hopefully) has enough money to pay people for their services, it can pay part or all of the salary and reduce, or eliminate, the accumulation of slices. This isn't the same things as buying back slices; it just reduces the amount of additional slices the person would deserve going forward. For instance, if you paid $20,000 of a fair market salary of $50,000, the person would be risking $30,000. The more cash you pay, the less risk the person takes and the fewer slices are allocated for the time she contributes. If you pay 100% of their fair market salary they would contribute zero slices.

Once you agree on the fair market salary for your job, you will want to convert the annual salary into an hourly rate. Do this by dividing the entire amount by 2,000, which is roughly the number of working hours in a year (40 hours times 50 weeks). I'm assuming at least two weeks of vacation time here.

On a side note, I recommend an open vacation policy. This means people can take as much time off as they need as long as their work is getting done. This not only treats people like adults who can manage their own time, but it also avoids the problem of managing slices for paid time off.

Built-In Incentives

One thing to notice is that *Slicing Pie* automatically rewards extra work if you are using the hourly rate. So, if someone works 50 hours per week they will contribute slices for 50 hours of work instead of 40 hours (a full-time work week in the US). *Slicing Pie* provides incentive for putting in the extra work as necessary.

However, this *only* applies to the at-risk portion of the salary. The paid portion of the salary does not reward extra work in the same way. In addition to rewarding extra time, this provides a *dis*incentive to take cash from the company, which is what you want if you're trying to conserve cash.

Overtime

If the participant's position or fair market salary makes them eligible for overtime payments, the model will apply the formula to these payments as well.

Pie Slicer

The Pie Slicer will automatically do the hourly calculation. Enter the *unpaid* portion of the annual salary on the Team Member settings page.

When and if you start paying someone, try to pay them in regular increments and deduct the annualized value of these payments from the base salary when you change the salary in the Pie Slicer.

For instance, if someone has a fair market salary of $50,000 and you pay them $1,000 per month, reduce the salary setting in the Pie Slicer by $12,000. The Pie Slicer will now use the new at-risk salary ($38,000) to calculate future slices. It will not retrofit slices already calculated.

If payments will be unpredictable you can use a Lump-Sum payment which will reduce slices starting with those from cash contributions.

In most cases, the amount of time people spend on the startup varies dramatically. It is not uncommon for some founders to spend 80 hours a week while others spend less than 10 as they juggle startup work with their day jobs. It is for this reason that you have to create an hourly rate. Participants simply track the hours they spend working to determine the fair market rate of their contribution of time. In "real" jobs you don't track your hours, you just work as much as you need. We use hours tracking for *Slicing Pie* to provide the right incentives and align people's interests.

Fair Market Value of Time = Hours x Hourly Rate
(plus overtime, if applicable)

You can also calculate a Slices Per Hour which will show you how many slices you contribute with every hour you contribute:

Slices Per Hour = Hourly Rate x Non-Cash Multiplier

This is the part of the program that some people find concerning (sometimes). The first thing that people don't like about this calculation is the thought of tracking their time. Most people, including me, *don't* like tracking their time. However, few things will give you better insight into what is going on with your startup company than a time report. If you don't know what people are spending time on, then you probably don't have a good handle on your business.

Most time-tracking systems, including the online Pie Slicer, will ask for notes on what was done during the time logged. Your time log reports are an *excellent* coaching tool for helping people to better manage their time and become more productive.

Not long ago, I spoke to an entrepreneur who was frustrated with his company's inability to generate revenue—a common complaint among startups. Because he was using the *Slicing Pie* model, he had fairly detailed records of his time. A quick review of the reports showed that very little of the teams' time had been spent on selling. Most of their time had been spent on development, customer service, research and other administrative tasks. They turned their attention to getting out and selling and within a few weeks they had some new customers. Without a good understanding of how time was being spent, this guy may still be scratching his head.

Another awesome side benefit to tracking time and other contributions is that it provides great information for professional investors during the due diligence process. Imagine how great it will be when you can show them *exactly* who did what and how much was spent. Traditional equity splits create animosity, whereas *Slicing Pie* creates a documented, logical record of a company's cap table.

The next thing that people worry about with regard to time-tracking is the *productivity* of the time spent. People are afraid that an unscrupulous coworker can simply log a bunch of hours and not do any work.

Time reports will not only tell you what someone is focusing on, but how productive they are. If someone is taking a lot of time to do simple tasks, you have a *management* issue with that person; it is not a flaw in the *Slicing Pie* model. If you have a chronic time-waster, you may have grounds for termination with cause (more on this later). Therefore, in the *Slicing Pie* model time tracking actively discourages time-wasting rather than encouraging it.

Value

On the flip side of the low productivity concern is the concern that time doesn't equal value. And, people with more experience may be more valuable than less experienced people. Remember that a contribution is what it is. Time spent on a startup does not magically make it more valuable. You are expected to perform at the same level for a startup that you would be for a real job. More experienced people usually have a higher hourly rate, which encapsulates their skills, education and expertise. You pay more for good employees because they can produce more for less money. You also pay more for good employees because they are supposed to come up with more great ideas than other employees.

The next major concern I hear about time tracking is the concern that there is much more to building value in a company than simply logging hours. That is true, but without time-tracking you will never understand one person's contribution relative to another. One person may work full time and another just a few hours per week. Unless you want to *guess* what each person is doing you should keep track.

You don't have to account for *every* minute of *every* day. As I mentioned before, you and your team can decide how much granularity you will accept. Some teams may be comfortable with a monthly entry that says "120 hours: did stuff," while others may want more detail. I personally like to know what people did with the time they spent.

If you still have a problem with time tracking, then you'll have to figure out some other way to accurately measure the fair market value of a person's time. I've heard lots of ideas; so far, not one works as well as time tracking!

Pie Slicer

When time is logged in the Pie Slicer, the user will have the option to choose a Project to which the time was dedicated. Project names are set up under the Pie settings menu.

Raises and Bonus Payments

If you have an employee that has lots of good ideas, they will be more valuable to your company and may deserve a raise, just like they would if they were working for a company that was paying them a cash salary.

Similarly, it's okay to negotiate a bonus if bonuses are typical for the type of position you are hiring for. Marketing executives may expect a bonus, but burger flippers may not. A good bonus program should be tied to company performance. A bonus program may not make sense for a company that isn't making money.

 **Pie Slicer**

To pay a bonus in Slices using the Pie Slicer, select the "Other" option from the Add Contribution pull-down menu.

Contractor Time

If the person isn't an employee, founder, partner, advisor or other long-term participant in your company they may be a contractor or freelancer. Startups often engage contractors and freelancers to work on specific projects. The hourly rate of a contract or freelance employee is likely to be much higher than their fair market salary. An individual who might be able to secure a job for $40,000 per year or $20 per hour might easily command $50 per hour as a freelance employee. This is normal because they have to make a living on fewer hours (to accommodate hours spent selling and admin work). Also, employers get the benefit of avoiding things like employment taxes (sometimes), benefits, and other expenses associated with long-term employees.

The fair market rate for these people is their hourly rate. However, it is fair to negotiate a buyout for the company so that the managers can avoid an absentee owner (this is someone who owns part of your company, but is no longer involved). I recommend a payment schedule that increases the buyout price to 200% of the base price. This means that if you *can* pay them, you *do* pay them; but if you can't, you would add their slices to the pie.

You would maintain the right to buy back the slices if you suddenly came into the money, according to the following schedule:

Month	Buyout	Month	Buyout
1	100%	7	155%
2	109%	8	164%
3	118%	9	173%
4	127%	10	182%
5	136%	11	191%
6	145%	12	200%

At the end of a year, you can buy them out for twice what they would have billed a regular client for their work. After that, the buyout option goes away for any billings more than a year old. You may still be able to come to an agreement, but you shouldn't *force* them to sell.

Fair Market Value of Time = Hours x Rate

To be clear, the fair market rate is used to calculate slices in the calculation above, not the buyout price. Think about it this way: a normal employee charges an annual rate and gets the benefit of being able to keep his slices (subject to termination rules). A contract employee charges a contract rate and, in exchange for a higher rate, is subject to a buyback. At the end of a year the company can't force a buyback.

If the contractor is going to be working with you over an extended period of time, it would be better to negotiate a fair market salary and include them as an employee, rather than a contractor. Because contractor rates are so much higher than full-time rates it's not fair to the other employees. Use contractors for limited engagements.

Not all contractors will go for a buyout option. They may not even want a slice of the company. You'll have to find a contractor that shares your vision and enthusiasm. Keep looking, they're out there!

🥧 Pie Slicer

Add the contractor as a regular contributor and set the salary by annualizing the hourly rate, which is Hourly Rate x 2,000. The contractor's slices will be added to the Pie. When, and if, you buy them out, you can simply delete their contribution under the contributions tab.

Ideas

It is not uncommon for people who have ideas to think they are entitled to a big chunk of equity just for having the idea. The instinct to want to benefit handsomely from "your baby" is real and it's very common. In the context of fairness, however, slices are only given when the fair market value is put at risk, and the way to determine the fair market value of the idea is to determine what kind of compensation an inventor would otherwise receive. In the non-startup world, an inventor of an idea often receives a *royalty* on revenues. Inventors, authors, and musicians routinely collect royalty checks as compensation for their ideas.

Royalties generally apply to "the" idea that is the idea upon which a company is founded. Ideas generated "on the job" usually don't get royalties. If you work for a company, coming up with great ideas is part of your job.

The *Slicing Pie* model uses the fair market value of unpaid royalties to calculate slices.

Fair Market Value of Ideas = Royalty Rate x Revenue Generated from Ideas

This assumes, of course, that the revenue generated can be directly attributed to the idea. If my publisher sells one of my books, for instance, I receive a royalty. If the same publisher sells a book from some other author, I don't. I might *enjoy* receiving a royalty on other people's intellectual property, but that wouldn't be fair. On second thought, knowing that it's not fair would take all the fun out of it, so I wouldn't actually want the royalty from someone else's book. Fair is more fun.

Sometimes, a lump-sum advance, may be appropriate. An advance is a chunk of slices from which future royalty payments will be deducted until the advance is paid back, then regular royalty payments can be made (in slices). In order for an advance to be warranted, the inventor should be the kind of person who earns advances. For instance, I, personally, can get advances from publishing companies, but a first-time author may not. So, if I gave you my book idea I should probably get an advance in slices.

Not every idea deserves a royalty. The idea has to enable a business to generate revenue and create a competitive advantage. For this to be true, the idea has to be good and unique enough that it creates some sort of "ownable" intellectual property, usually in the form of a patent or copyright. Starting a hamburger stand might be a good idea, but it's not unique enough in itself to create a sustainable competitive advantage. In the case of a hamburger stand, the *execution* may create a sustainable advantage, not the idea.

If, however, you invent a single-polarity magnet that can create unlimited energy, you can probably secure a patent and the patent can create a sustainable competitive advantage. This idea, therefore, is the kind of idea for which the originator deserves slices.

In some cases, the time and money spent developing the idea before the company started could be translated into slices using the relevant calculations. In these cases, the development of the idea would be part of the development of the company and the royalty would not apply.

 **Pie Slicer**

Set the Royalty Rate under the Pie Settings menu. Log relevant sales in the sales dialog box and the Pie Slicer will calculate the royalties.

Relationships

A well-connected person can do wonders for a startup by bringing the right relationships. Relationships are so important to startups that people usually wind up *overpaying* when using traditional equity splits because they are desperate. Similar to idea people, people with good relationships tend to want chunks of equity upfront. Like ideas, relationships are valuable when and if they generate revenue, investment or other financial benefit. In the *Slicing Pie* model, there are simple ways to calculate the fair market value.

A well-connected person who simply makes introductions may not deserve slices. But a person who can help convert them into value certainly does. Relationships turn into value when they lead to revenues, investments, or other formal relationships with the company.

Customers

When relationships turn into sales, the individual responsible for the sale is generally entitled to a sales commission on the revenue generated. Rates will vary by industry, but a commission of 5%-10% is typical. Pay the rate that is appropriate for your industry and make sure you pay the same commission to all salespeople.

Fair Market Value = Revenue x Commission Rate (%)

Not *every* person in your company will be entitled to a commission. A commissioned salesperson will usually receive a sales commission in addition to a base salary, which is often smaller than others in the firm at a similar level. Founders and other senior managers do not generally take a commission, for instance. Advisors usually don't take commission either. In some cases, you can provide one commission rate on the initial sale and a lower commission rate on subsequent sales. Whoever is responsible for generating the revenue deserves the commission. If someone hands your salesperson a business card from someone they met at a party and your salesperson does all the work, your salesperson deserves the Pie. Similarly, if someone introduces your salesperson to a lifelong friend, but the salesperson does the rest, the salesperson still deserves the reward. Only offer slices to individuals who drive sales. A casual introduction probably isn't good enough.

🥧 Pie Slicer

Commission rates are set under the Pie Settings options.

The user or the Pie owner will have to enter the Revenue for that period in the Sales dialog box. The Pie slicer will calculate the slices in lieu of a paid commission.

It's important to determine, in advance, when you are going to recognize the sale. Some companies may want to do it at the time of the sale. Others may want to wait until the cash is actually collected. I recommend entering sales on a monthly basis and only counting cash collected during the month. Unless you are disciplined about this process, you will run the risk of inaccurate allocations.

Investors

Similar to generating revenue, when someone's relationship creates a new investment, that person would be entitled to a finder's fee. But again, they should do more than just make an introduction; they should stay active throughout the process as needed.

A typical finder's fee would be 5% for the first $1,000,000 and 2.5% for every million after that.

**Fair Market Value = (First Million x 5%)
+ (The Rest x 2.5%)**

You may run into legal issues with the finder's fee. In some cases, only a registered broker can collect a finder's fee. Check with a *Slicing Pie*-friendly attorney. Finder's fees are much less common than sales commissions. If your company is uncomfortable paying the finder's fee then you might consider paying a one-time spot bonus or something similar instead.

Pie Slicer

The **Add Funds to Well** screen gives the user the option of choosing the team member who should receive the fee. Only one fee per investment is allowed. The fee is calculated in slices.

The Finder's Fee is set in the Pie Settings options.

You can also add a Finder's Fee for people who find investors whose money will not go into the Well. For instance, a regular convertible loan would not go into the Well, but the Finder's Fee may still be appropriate.

Partners & Vendors

It is not common (at least in the United States) to provide compensation for finding partners or vendors. For the most part, this is just part of the job we are hired to do.

In some cases, however, the partner or vendor will provide some sort of reward. For instance, a printing company might provide a sales commission to a person who helped them close a deal. If the partner paid the commission the company may not want to pay as well. I prefer not to provide slices in exchange for relationships that turn into partnerships or vendors, but it's up to you!

If a partnership or vendor produces measurable savings over a previous solution, you can allocate a percentage of the savings (under 5%) to the person who helped find the vendor.

Fair Market Value = ~5% x Savings or one-time bonus or nothing

Employees

Sometimes, a relationship will turn into a new hire. In these cases, a referral fee may be appropriate. Choose an amount you are comfortable with and offer it to anyone who refers an employee. Typically, you would wait at least six months before providing the slices, so you will have time to make sure the employee sticks around!

$250 to $500 is a good place to start. Referral fees are quite common in the United States and can be a great way to reward current employees for participating in the recruitment process.

Fair Market Value = Referral Fee

🕸 Pie Slicer

Select **"Other"** from the Add Contribution menu to log bonuses and Referral Fees. In most cases, these will be treated as Non-Cash because the team member did not spend their own money.

Facilities

These days, there is plenty of unused office and warehouse space that startups can move into. Most startups are willing to put up with less-than-perfect conditions, so there are lots of choices.

If someone contributes office or warehouse space, they would receive slices instead of rent. The fair market value is equal to the amount of money the space would command on the open market if there was a willing tenant.

It's important to note that the startup should only pay (in slices) for the space that is needed for the startup. If the landlord gives them 20 offices and they only need four, they should only have to pay for four.

Fair Market Value = Market Rate Rent for Space Used

Summary

The fair market rate of many non-cash contributions is observable in the marketplace. When people don't get paid a fair market rate for non-cash contributions they are putting the unpaid portion at risk.

To calculate slices contributed from non-cash contributions, determine the fair market value of the contribution and multiply by the non-cash multiplier (I recommend two).

Unlike cash contributions, non-cash contributions do not incur out-of-pocket costs and are usually easier to come by. Therefore, they get a lower multiplier.

Additional Reading

You may already be in a startup with a fixed split. Have no fear! You can retrofit the *Slicing Pie* model to determine what your split should look like. The retrofit chapter goes into more detail!

Chapter Seven:

Recovery Framework

Absentee owners are individuals who own part of a company, but are no longer actively involved. This is sometimes referred to as "dead" equity. Professional investors tend to avoid investing in companies with too many absentee owners, so the company needs a mechanism to recover shares or slices from people who leave the company.

As you will see, the multipliers/normalizers in the *Slicing Pie* model create consequences for individuals when they make decisions that adversely affect the company and vice versa. These consequences provide protection for both parties and, in many ways, are the "secret sauce" that makes the *Slicing Pie* method so effective and fair.

The recovery framework applies to just about anyone who separates from the company. There are a couple of exceptions for contractors and advisors, but for the most part, in *Slicing Pie* everyone gets the same treatment whether you call them a founder, partner, employee, or anything else. In this chapter I will refer to the person being separated as an employee.

Nature of the Separations

The recovery of the slices is dependent upon both the nature of the separation and the nature of the relationship with the individual.

There are four primary reasons an individual would separate from a company:

A. Fired for Good Reason
B. Fired for No Good Reason
C. Resigned for Good Reason
D. Resigned for No Good Reason

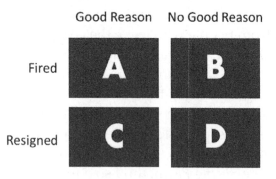

These terms, and their following definitions, are very similar to those commonly found in American employment agreements. The terminology may be slightly different, however. "Fired for Good Reason" might be called "Terminated for Cause," for instance. In the UK the terms "Good Leaver" and "Bad Leaver" are common.

Fired for Good Reason

Being fired for good reason (sometimes called "for cause") means that the employee's *behavior* led to a management decision to fire the person. Performance-related issues are the most common. But, if there is a performance issue, the individual must be given a chance to correct their behavior. I recommend *at least two warnings* with a clear outline of the performance issue and what needs to be done to correct it. It's *not fair* to fire someone for performance-related issues without first giving them the chance to correct their behavior. After all, they may not know what they are doing wrong. Or they may not know the impact their behavior is having on the firm.

Other good reasons to fire someone would be stealing, sexual harassment, threatening coworkers, drug abuse, and other extreme behavior.

When an employee is fired for good reason, their decisions negatively impact the company. Consequently, they will *lose* any slices allocated from contributions *except* supplies, equipment and cash contributions which would be recalculated *without* the multipliers. Additionally, the company has the right (but, not the obligation) to buy back the equity in an amount of cash equal to the outstanding slices.

Lastly, the employee should agree not to compete directly with the company or cause the other employees to leave. It doesn't matter if a non-compete or non-solicitation isn't enforceable by law in your market, it's not fair to be fired and then go work for a direct competitor or steal employees.

In this case, removing the multipliers has created a consequence for the employee. Knowing that this is the consequence forces employees to think twice before slacking off and hurting the company, or choosing to engage in other negative behaviors.

If this seems harsh, remember that startups are fragile businesses and they can't afford to have deadbeat employees who do bad things.

Fired for No Good Reason

On the flip side, if the employee is fired through no fault of their own (also called "without cause"), they get to *keep* all their slices. The company can offer to buy the slices back in an amount of cash equal to the outstanding slices, but the employee should not be obligated to sell.

In this case, the company has to deal with the inconvenience of having "dead" equity or buying it back at a very high premium. Keeping the multipliers has created a consequence for the company, forcing the management team to think twice before letting someone go for no reason. This protects the employee from the decisions made by the management team that negatively impact their future.

I've both heard and experienced equity horror stories where managers fire employees for the sole purpose of getting back equity. In many cases such transactions are perfectly legal, but being legal isn't the same thing as being fair. If a management team terminates an employee through no fault of their own they should be prepared to face consequences that include compensating the employee for the risk they accepted by participating in the startup.

There are a number of reasons a person would be fired for no good reason, including a change in strategy, reduction in force, elimination of redundant positions, or "just because". Most jobs (at least in the U.S.) are considered "at will", meaning the company can fire anyone, for any reason, at any time.

The company can't prevent the individual from going to work for a competitor either. It's not fair to fire someone for no reason and then limit their job prospects. This doesn't mean the person can steal ideas and customers, but it does mean they can go join the competition. However, the company *would* be within their right to ask for a non-solicitation agreement which prevents the employee from hiring the company's employees within a specified period of time (usually one year).

Resign for Good Reason

Sometimes, a company doesn't outright fire someone, but they make decisions that essentially "push" an employee out. There are well-documented legal reasons as to why a person would be entitled to resign for "good reason" (also called "for cause") that are often found in employment contracts. The employee wouldn't *have* to leave, but they can if their job is clearly no longer what they signed up for. If they stay, however, they can't use these as good reasons later on. The good reasons include:

✓ *Adverse change in title or responsibilities.* If the Vice President of Marketing was demoted to the Head Burger Flipper, the person would have a good reason to leave.

✓ *Adverse change in compensation that does not affect other participants at the same level.* If the management team cuts the individual's salary or raises their own by a significant amount, but does not take similar action against others at the same level.

✓ *Relocation of the company more than 50 miles from its original location.* The person may not be able to manage the commute. Extending the commute puts an unfair burden on the employee.

✓ *Death or disability.* This happens, unfortunately.

✓ *Adoption of the Slicing Pie model after a fixed-split agreement is in place.* If you're retrofitting *Slicing Pie* a person may want out of the deal. In fact, *any* unexpected change of a person's equity would be good reason.

✓ *Changes to Pie Settings.* This, in effect, changes the compensation program.

Leaving a company for good reason is essentially the same as being fired for no good reason. The employee gets to keep all their slices. The company can offer to buy the slices back for an amount of cash equal to the outstanding slices, but the employee should not be obligated to sell. They should not be asked to agree to a non-compete.

Again, the multipliers impose consequences on the company, forcing them to be careful about the decisions they make that impact employees. However, they can ask for a non-solicitation agreement as described above.

Resign for No Good Reason

The last reason for separation is when someone quits for their own reasons unrelated to the firm. Perhaps they no longer believe in the company's vision, perhaps they found a better job somewhere else, or perhaps they won the lottery and want to retire. It may be a good reason for *them*, but not for the *company*. No matter what the reason, they are leaving a company that needs them and will have to suffer the consequences, which are the same as being fired for good reason. They will *lose* any slices allocated from contributions *except* supplies, equipment and cash contributions which would be recalculated *without* the multipliers. The company may buy back the slices if they have the money and a non-compete/non-solicitation agreement would be appropriate. This is the same consequence as being fired for good reason. If employees make choices that adversely impact the company, they have to suffer the consequences.

Loyal Employees

Sometimes, a loyal employee works hard, but has to resign to make ends meet. It's true that they may be leaving the company in the lurch, but taking back their equity may not seem like the right thing to do. In these cases, I recommend the person reduce their hours, but stay involved on a part-time basis. This will allow them to keep their slices and allow the company to continue to benefit from their expertise.

You could also adopt a rule which states that any slices over a certain number of months or a pre-set percentage stay in place in the event of resignation with no good reason. (You can specify this on the form at the beginning of this book and in the Pie Slicer settings.) This will give good employees who have to leave an option to do so without losing everything. I think it's important to have *some* consequences, but I understand that people's personal lives may not always stay compatible with working with a startup.

I do not recommend doing this for people who are fired for good reason. It's best to sever ties completely with someone who may have left on anything but amicable terms.

Buyout Price

The *Slicing Pie* model will tell you the fair buyout price so you won't overpay or underpay. The price will be the number of outstanding slices times the currency rate. So, if the terminated participant has 1,000 slices and your fund is operating in dollars, the buyout price is $1,000.

When you buy someone out who was terminated for good reason or resigned for no good reason you are essentially paying them back for cash and tangible contributions. Their "investment" of time, money and other contributions didn't pay off, which is fine because leaving was their fault or choice anyway.

However, when you buy someone out who was terminated for no good reason or resigned for good reason, they get compensated for the risk they took. They are getting what they would have been paid on the open market times the multipliers. This provides a nice rate of return.

Traditionally buyout prices are negotiated when the employee leaves. This requires everyone to *guess* what the current price is and inevitably leads to arguments about valuation. The *Slicing Pie* buyout price *does not* imply a valuation; it simply implies a fair settlement.

It's not uncommon for the people who are bought out to be the only people who walk away with anything from the startup. This is because startups pay people who leave the company and then the company goes out of business, leaving the people who stayed with nothing. This may be unavoidable, but with *Slicing Pie*, you will never overpay!

On-The-Job Buyouts

In some cases, the company can offer to buy back slices from participants even though they are staying with the company.

If the company uses company money to buy back an individual's slices, the slices will vanish from the money and the Pie will recalculate everyone else's shares, which means they will all have a higher percentage. When someone sells slices back to the company they are getting a chunk of money and forgoing a share of future profits.

Company Offers

If the company has the cash, managers can offer to buyout slices at the current rate ($1 per slice in the US). Remember, this doesn't mean slices are "worth" something, it is just means to compensate people for taking a risk and providing a means to put cash in their pockets.

It's important to note, while I recommend $1/slice, the company can certainly offer more or less than that. The employee can take it or leave it. The company can make any offer it wants, it just can't force a buyback.

Employee Requests

If an employee needs cash, they can *request* a buyout. This is different from a company offer because if the employee is making the request, they are essentially "backing out" of the deal and removing their at-risk contributions. *If* the company has the money, it can provide lump-sum payments which will reduce the employee's at-risk contributions—starting with cash contributions—up to their total at-risk contributions. You will have to recalculate their slices after paying them.

Sometimes employees need the money or can't tolerate the risk associated with startups. There is nothing wrong with this and providing these payments may enable the company to retain people who might otherwise resign.

Be careful, however, that the employee isn't simply trying to get paid before quitting. Paying someone just to have them quit is not in the spirit of *Slicing Pie*. Consider waiting before making payments or paying in installments.

🌟 Pie Slicer

To remove a contributor, click the little gear to the upper right of their profile image to open the Team Member Settings dialog box. The Pie Slicer will ask you to specify the circumstances of their separation and apply the appropriate calculations.

Their slices will remain in the Pie until they are bought out.

To buy out a team member, click on the Summary tab. The Pie Slicer will show the buyout price next to the team member. Clicking the bubble will remove the individual and their slices from the Pie.

You may need to account for the transaction by adding the buyout expense to another team member or drawing funds from the Well. The Pie Slicer will not do this automatically.

Claw Back

As mentioned before, when someone resigns for good reason, or is fired for no good reason, the company can offer to buy them back at an amount equal to the outstanding slices that were calculated with the multipliers. This represents a very nice return on the individual's investment of both cash and non-cash contributions. Most people *hope* they will receive a lot more, but the multipliers provide a fair return, given the risk.

However, it's not fair for the company to buy back the slices and then turn around and sell the company for a far better return. If a transaction takes place *within a year* of a buyout that would have led to higher return, the person should be paid the difference. This is known as "claw back" and it prevents the managers from firing everyone, buying back their slices at one price, and then selling the company at a higher price.

If the person was fired for good reason or resigned for no good reason, the claw back would not apply. Talk to your *Slicing Pie*-friendly lawyer about claw back.

Caveats

As I alluded to earlier, there are a number of important caveats that could impact the way people are treated on the way out the door. Remember, *Slicing Pie* is about doing right by the people who help you succeed and it's important to clarify a few things to prevent one group of people from inadvertently taking advantage of others.

Advisory Board Members

Because advisors are usually successful people who may have acquired some wealth, they may have unusually high fair market salaries. So high, in fact, that it may not be practical to pay them such a high rate. I recommend capping their hourly compensation at 200 slices/hour and asking them to contribute at least ten hours before cutting them in. For this, they enjoy the benefit of being *immune to termination* as described above.

Unless there were extenuating circumstances, you wouldn't be able to fire an advisor who took the capped hourly slices option. Instead, you would simply stop going to them for advice and they would simply stop earning slices. However, you would not be able to erase their slices if you fired them. So, when it comes to advisory board members, there is rarely such thing as termination for cause. Advisors would typically keep their shares with the multipliers.

However, if they told you they no longer wanted to work with you, this is the equivalent of resignation for no good reason and you could recover their slices.

If the advisor does not want the slices cap then you have the option of giving them a rate that more accurately reflects their market rate, but they wouldn't enjoy the benefit of protection against termination.

✹ Pie Slicer

The Pie Slicer will not allow you to terminate an advisor.

Investors

Friends and family investors who put cash into the Well can't really be fired either as long as their primary role is investment. They would keep their slices with the multipliers, no matter what happens. You could offer to buy them out with the

4x multiplier (which would be a nice return), but they shouldn't be forced to sell.

If an investor *wants* their money back they can ask for it, which is the same thing as resignation for no reason. In these cases, you would have to pay them back without the multiplier if and when you can afford it.

Contractors

If you are using a contractor schedule as outlined earlier, the termination rules would not apply. Once the contractor's slices are accounted for, you can't fire them and get the slices back.

You can, however, offer to buy back slices or pay them if they request payment as outlined above.

Rent and Royalties

If a terminated participant is entitled to a royalty for their intellectual property, they will continue to contribute slices unless the company pays the royalty in cash.

Similarly, if the terminated participant owns the facilities they will continue to contribute slices unless the company starts paying rent.

Summary

When an individual separates from a company, it may be in the company's best interest to recover slices, if they can, to avoid having absentee owners, aka "dead equity."

The multipliers in the *Slicing Pie* model create consequences for the at-fault party. If the company makes decisions that adversely impact the future of an individual employee, the result will be employees who resign for good reason or who are fired for no good reason. Consequently, it is expensive to get slices back from them and the company cannot *force* a sale, nor can the company expect the employee to agree to non-competition. In these cases, the employee would retain all their slices in the pie and the company could offer to buy them back, but the employee should not be obligated to sell. Additionally, a claw-back provision should be included with any sale that allows the employee to benefit from the full price of the shares in the event the company is sold at a higher price within a year.

Conversely, if the employee makes decisions that adversely impact the future of the company, the result would be termination with good reason or resignation without good reason. In these cases the employee would *lose* their slices, except those contributed with equipment, supplies and cash, which would be recalculated *without* the multipliers. Additionally, the company should expect the employee to adhere to a non-compete agreement. If the company has the money, they can force a buyout without the benefit of the claw-back provision.

In all cases, the company should expect the employee to adhere to a non-solicitation agreement which prevents them from luring the company's employees away.

Chapter Eight:

Freezing the Pie

The combination of the allocation and recovery frameworks provides a universal structure for awarding equity or profit sharing in a bootstrapped startup. By agreeing to the rules in advance, and holding all participants accountable to the rules, each participant is treated fairly and their risk is properly recognized.

The *Slicing Pie* model is best suited for early-stage companies who don't have much cash. As the company grows and develops, it will start generating cash and profits (hopefully). When that starts to happen, it can simply pay for everything it needs and the model will stop allocating new slices. It will, in effect, "freeze" and the ownership of the participants will no longer change. (Your attorney may call this "termination.") When and if the company distributes profits, the model will tell you how much each person gets.

Below is the diagram from earlier in the book:

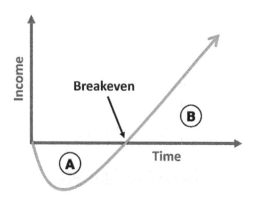

Slicing Pie considers the fair market value of the at-risk contributions represented by area A. When the company reaches breakeven everyone is getting paid or reimbursed for expenses. No more "bets" are placed and the Pie will terminate, or freeze. At this point, you and the team will have a traditional fixed split which is okay because the Pie won't change anyway unless you implement an equity bonus/incentive program (the topic of another book!)

Area B represents the income generated. If the company pays dividends, each person will get a share of those dividends based on the final split. Ta-da!

In some cases, a company will not actually breakeven, but instead will raise Series A investment. This event will also freeze the Pie because the individual participants aren't placing more bets. The company has now become an investment tool.

Here is how the freezing scenario will unfold:

Revenue

The *Slicing Pie* model *always* aligns people's incentives so that they make the right kind of decisions. Managers and employees will be aligned in their interests to get to cash flow breakeven as soon as they can so they can freeze their share. In a fixed split model it doesn't really matter when the company gets to breakeven because it won't impact shares.

As the company begins to generate revenue, the management team can choose how to reinvest the revenue into the company. This means they can use the money to pay for contributions instead of using slices. This reduces how much each person puts at risk.

The best use of company funds is to use them to pay for things that would have otherwise consumed cash from the Well or to reimburse employees for expenses. When cash from the Well or an employee is consumed, it converts to slices using the higher cash multiplier, making it "expensive" relative to non-cash contributions.

When the out-of-pocket cash needs of the company are met, the management team can use what's left to start paying for non-cash contributions such as rent, commissions, royalties and salaries. The amount paid towards the fair market rate for these contributions will reduce the number of slices allocated for that input. If the company pays 100% of the fair market rate for the contribution, there is no need to calculate additional slices.

At this point—when the company is paying for everything—the model will no longer allocate slices for contributions and the model will *stop* changing. It will stay frozen unless the company's financial situation requires it to use more slices, instead of cash, in the future.

A frozen pie is a good thing. In fact, it's *the point* of your work! This means the people who worked to get the company to breakeven and beyond will each have what they deserve to have and will, as you will see below, share in the profits of the company. When new members come on board you can pay them their market rate and you won't have to feel obligated to give them slices at all.

Profits

When the company is paying 100% of its expenses it will generate profits. After the IRS takes their fair share, the company can either save the money so it can invest in the company in the future (aka "retained earnings") or distribute the profits to shareholders (aka "dividends"). When and if dividends are paid, the Pie will determine how much everyone gets.

Profit distributions are made after all other financial obligations have been met. This includes fair market salaries. This means that each participant will not only get their fair market salary, but also they will receive their fair share of the profits when and if the company decides to distribute profits. I hope your profits far exceed your fair market salaries!

If someone joined the company *after* the company could afford to pay, they would get their fair market salary and would not get a portion of the profits. This is fair because they did not take any risk. They can participate in the company's bonus program going forward.

This can happen in perpetuity. Participants can continue to enjoy their fair market salary and a portion of the profits that properly reflects the contribution they made before the company could pay.

Recovery

Although no more slices are being allocated, the rules of the recovery framework will still apply. However, if you are using a "loyal employee" option as described above, an employee leaving for no reason might retain their equity depending on how long ago they earned it.

Person-to-Person Sales

If person A buys person B's slices the slices will transfer to person A, so person A will get the profit distributions, when and if payments are made. In other words, the slices do not vanish; they stay in the pie but belong to someone else. Your company can decide whether or not you will allow these kinds of transactions. It would be smart to check with your lawyer to make sure it's legal in your area!

Of course, more established companies may warrant a value that exceeds the *Slicing Pie* model value. In these cases, the fair market value should be used, not the *Slicing Pie* model per slice buyout price. Your company's managers will determine whether they will allow one participant to sell slices to another. I personally think it's okay (as long as it's a legal transaction). I recommend that you avoid selling to people who are not actively involved in the company, however. This will create an absentee owner situation, which isn't great.

Series A Investment

If your company cannot get to profitability on its own, or if it needs money for growth, it will have to raise money from outside investors. Any investment that covers a part, but not all, of the company's cash requirements is an angel investment and should be treated as a convertible note, SAFE (simple agreement for future equity) or as a loan and included in the Well as described earlier. However, when a substantial amount of money is raised that *will* meet the cash needs of the company in the foreseeable future, this is a "Series A" investment. (More later in the chapter about financing the pie). At this point, you can freeze/terminate the Pie and all participants will be subject to the terms of the Series A investors. These people will likely be professional investors with professional term sheets that outline all sorts of things.

One of the most important things the term sheet will outline is the valuation of the company. This will determine the underlying value of the shares. This has *nothing* to do with the number of slices in the pie and everything to do with how good your management team is at negotiating a healthy valuation. If you have good employees, provide good value, and (most importantly) have real traction showing a predictable marketing model, you should be able to negotiate a high price.

Summary

When the company generates revenue, it can use the revenue to pay for the things it needs. Paying for part of the cost will *reduce* the number of slices the model will allocate. Paying for *all* of the costs will *eliminate* the allocation of slices and the model will stop changing.

When revenue surpasses expenses, it will generate profits. The model will determine the distribution of these profits if the management team decides to distribute them.

If the company needs cash prior to breakeven it can raise enough money to meet its financial obligations in the foreseeable future. This is a Series A investment and the new investors will take equity based on the negotiated value. All participants in the company will be subject to the terms and conditions of the Series A investors.

The termination rules will stay in effect until the management decides to change them.

After the Pie terminates, bonus programs can be used to provide incentives for employees.

Additional Reading

If you are ready to raise money for your startup, or if you are ramping up sales revenue, you may want to check out another one of my books, *Pitch Ninja*, which covers a method for delivering a very persuasive presentation. For more information, just visit **www.pitch.ninja**

Chapter Nine:

Financing the Pie

Slicing Pie is a financing tool for founders who don't have access to a lot of cash. If a founder *does* have access to a lot of cash, they do not need *Slicing Pie*. They can just pay for everything and keep all the equity for themselves. Unfortunately, many founders aren't flush with cash.

This chapter contains some thoughts on how various financing options work with the *Slicing Pie* model. As a rule, equity financing is "expensive" relative to debt financing. In other words, it's "cheaper" to borrow money than it is to use slices. However, borrowing money may leave you with debt if the company fails.

In general, the fewer slices in the Pie the better, as this keeps the denominator low in the *Slicing Pie* formula.

Bootstrapped companies with little access to cash need to be smart about how they use it. Some things can't be acquired with slices. For instance, the government won't want slices instead of corporate filing fees, and Google doesn't have a "Slices Per Click" advertising program (yet). You'll need cash for things like this and when you pay for them you will contribute four slices to the Pie for each dollar you spend.

The best way to conserve limited cash is by asking people to forgo compensation and contribute slices to the Pie instead. It breaks my heart to see a founder spend all their cash on developing a product and then not be able to market it!

Using cash to pay people dilutes the Pie. If a company is using my recommended multipliers and a founder, Daisy, pays a developer, Ty, $10,000 for creating an app, the Pie accumulates 40,000 slices (for Daisy). If, however, Ty forgoes the cash compensation, the Pie will only accumulate 20,000 slices (for Ty), and Daisy will still have $10,000 to put into marketing. The fewer slices in the Pie the better.

Whenever possible, avoid putting cash in people's pockets. If possible, use the money on things other than paying for people's time or non-cash contributions.

Founder Money

The first source of cash is from the coffers of early participants. At first, this money comes in the form of petty expenses that go unreimbursed. For these costs, the participant will contribute slices to the pie. Keeping track of early expenses is important so the founder can calculate slices.

Well Money

Soon, the company will begin to receive bills that it will want to pay from a company checking account instead of having individual participants cover the costs. As discussed before, the Well is a holding account for larger amounts of money contributed by participants. Well funders are usually participating members of the team, but sometimes this money comes from friends & family.

When the money is spent, slices will be accumulated in the Pie using the cash multiplier.

Personal Loans

As the company grows, it may need to make larger purchases or acquisitions. Debt financing may be a more appropriate way to finance these purchases, especially if the company is purchasing a tangible asset, like physical equipment or inventory.

Loans can come from anyone, even founders, but the company must pay back the loan. A typical loan has a market-rate interest payment and principal payment. The person who makes the loan *does not* get slices for loaning the money because the company is making payments. If the company *isn't* or *can't* make a payment, the unpaid portion of the payment will convert to four slices per dollar for the person who *is* paying the loan, or the person who made the loan but isn't getting payment. Each missed payment converts to slices.

Loan payments get paid as a regular expense of the company and, if the company is sold, loans get paid off *before* equity holders get disbursements.

Using debt financing helps reduce the overall number of slices in the Pie.

Bank Loans/Credit Cards

If you can get them, bank loans and credit cards are a source of funding, but someone will be on the hook for the full amount of the loan if the company goes under. Banks usually require a personal guarantee from founders and rarely finance startups without steady revenue.

If the company is making payments, the person who secured the loan does not get slices. However, if the person who secured the loan makes the payments the amount of the *payment* will convert at the cash rate.

Like personal loans, bank and credit card debt has priority over equity holders.

Unsecured banks loans, while rare, are the responsibility of the company and the bank will come after the company if it defaults.

Secured bank loans are treated the same as personal loans. Instead of taking the money from a savings account, the person borrowed money on personal credit. Remember, *Slicing Pie* doesn't care where the money comes from.

Convertible Notes/SAFE

One of the nice things about *Slicing Pie* is that you don't have to engage in a futile attempt to value your startup company. Never attempt to value your company unless you are raising a Series A round.

A convertible note is a loan that *converts* to equity at the same terms of the Series A investor. Similarly, a SAFE (simple agreement for future equity) also relies on the terms of the Series A investor. Do an internet search for more on how these agreements work.

In the *Slicing Pie* model, both SAFEs and convertible notes can be offered for investments from "arm's-length" angel investors instead of slices. An arm's-length angel is someone who is simply backing the company financially, and not taking an active role in advising or managing the company.

Remember, *Slicing Pie* relies on the fair market value for contributions. Transactions in the market for angel investments are often handled in this way. Angel investors are familiar and comfortable with these tools, but they may not be familiar with *Slicing Pie*. Offering convertible notes or a SAFE is perfectly legitimate.

Keep in mind that the terms of a SAFE or a convertible note are negotiable and may not always be in your best interest.

Some angel investors may ask for slices instead of a convertible note. If they take slices, they should adhere to the rules of *Slicing Pie*. Cash in the Pie should not carry special privileges. If an angel investor tries to impose special rights on top of *Slicing Pie,* tell them, "no," and find a new angel investor. I know it's hard to walk away from funding, but a bad deal will come back to haunt you.

Venture Capital

Startups that need $1,000,000+ often approach professional venture capitalists. These people invest in startups for a living and are usually investing OPM (other people's money). Because they aren't making *personal* bets on the future of your startup, they don't (and won't) accept slices in the Pie.

VCs participate in what's called a "priced round." This means that the founders and the investors have determined the price for a share of stock in the company. A priced round should be accompanied by the appropriate legal documentation. In the US, the document is called a Private Placement Memorandum (PPM).

The PPM contains all sorts of details about your company, the business you're in, the managers, the financials, the market and all the reasons you will probably *fail* in your business. A PPM helps prevent financial fraud and without a PPM, you run the risk of violating the law. This means that if you sell stock to your mom for a set price, you may be *breaking the law.*

Hiring lawyers to create a PPM is very expensive, so unless you are raising a lot of money, it's better to use the less expensive convertible note or a SAFE. These tools do not require a PPM or a valuation.

Series A is usually the first "officially" priced round followed by Series B, C, D, etc. Each round requires a new valuation and new offering documents.

When you approach the venture capitalist you should be prepared to show them a cap table. A cap table, or capitalization table, shows who owns equity in your company and how much in terms of a number of shares or percentages or both. VCs look for logical cap tables, a happy team and as few absentee owners as possible. *Slicing Pie* delivers just that!

Not every VC is familiar with the *Slicing Pie* model (yet) and some may ask questions. Tell them that the model allocates equity based on the fair market value of the contributions made. Feel free to give them a copy of this book or email me at mike@slicingpie.com and I'll send them a copy.

When a VC looks at your company they will have a lot of questions; this is called "due diligence". They will want to know how much time and money have been invested to date and who did what. If you're using *Slicing Pie*, you will have records of all this stuff so you won't have to remember everything. *Slicing Pie* makes due diligence a breeze and gives investors unparalleled insight to the team and company.

Summary

Different sources of funding are treated differently under the *Slicing Pie* model. When founders spend their own money, the Pie accumulates slices using the cash multiplier. Founders should make financing decisions that minimize the use of slices.

Debt financing can limit the number of slices if the company repays the loan's principal and pays interest.

For arm's-length angel investors, a convertible note or a SAFE may be a legitimate option. These tools do not contribute slices to the Pie and they delay reliance on a set valuation until the first priced round.

A priced round is usually led by a professional VC firm that invests other people's money in startup companies. Pricing the round carries expensive legal requirements, making valuations impractical during earlier rounds. Pricing a round without the proper documentation may be illegal.

VC's don't take slices in the Pie, but they will find *Slicing Pie* helpful because it delivers a clean cap table and the record-keeping in *Slicing Pie* makes due diligence much easier!

Chapter Ten:

Legal Issues

This chapter only covers high-level advice for implementing a *Slicing Pie* agreement. Remember, *I'm not a lawyer* and *I'm not trying to provide legal or tax advice.* I just want to provide some talking points for you and your lawyer.

I believe that *Slicing Pie* is a universal, one-size-fits-all solution for equity splits in early-stage, bootstrapped companies. As described above, the model applies until the company has enough money in the bank to simply pay for its expenses either from revenues generated or a Series A round of financing. When there is money in the bank, or coming in, that can cover foreseeable future expenses, the *Slicing Pie* model terminates and turns into a fixed split. At this point, each participant's risk is properly accounted for and, when the profits or sale comes, each participant will get what they deserve.

A Universal Slicing Pie Contract

My dream is to have a simple, inexpensive, one-size-fits-all legal agreement that any person on the planet can download and use for their own company. Unfortunately, my dream for a single contract may not come true because there are too many countries and states and complicated laws to make this happen - at least, not in the short term.

Slicing Pie-Friendly Attorneys

That being said, there are lawyers in a number of countries who offer *Slicing Pie* contracts and consultations at a very reasonable price. Getting your hands on one of these contracts and speaking to a *Slicing Pie*-friendly lawyer is a great place to start.

I have engaged attorneys all over the world who can help companies implement *Slicing Pie* and I'm always looking for new legal partners. When I find an attorney that understands and appreciates the benefits of the model, I will introduce them to readers or list their names on my site(s). I always look for legal partners who push clients to implement the model with as few changes as possible, and who are sensitive to the financial constraints of startups. There are lots of good ways to spend money on legal services. The less you need to spend on corporate formation and founder's agreements, the more you can spend on intellectual property, user agreements, customer contracts and other items that can help your company build value.

Most lawyers haven't read my books on the *Slicing Pie* model (yet) and, therefore, aren't well versed in the nuances of dynamic equity splits. They may not feel prepared to properly document the agreements. In some extreme cases they *may* try to talk you out of it. Do not be discouraged! People all over the world have successfully implemented this method, and there are numerous ways to implement it. Implementing the *Slicing Pie* model should be as quick and easy as a fixed split model and should *not* cost much more than any other corporate formation.

Change the Law

Some countries have more oppressive laws than others when it comes to startups. If you live in one of these countries, you should try to *change the laws*. People always chuckle when I say this in my live events, but I'm serious. If your legal environment is such that you can't even implement a fair equity split, you should bring this to the attention of the people who make laws and ask them to change it. Entrepreneurship is an important part of every economy on the planet. Countries usually want to encourage startups and I've seen sweeping changes in legal environments all over the world. *Slicing Pie* has been part of many of these conversations. I've even been sponsored by government agencies to come and speak about *Slicing Pie*.

Documenting the Deal

There is much more to a founder's agreement or operating agreement than *Slicing Pie*. A typical start-up contract should include the roles, rights and responsibilities of participants, how decisions get made, the ownership of intellectual property, and confidentiality policies. Even the purpose and goals of an organization can be addressed in a legal contract to help ensure that participants know what they're getting into.

Slicing Pie simply addresses the allocation and recovery of equity or profit sharing in a company, an important, but specific, part of the overall content of founding documents.

Applicable Laws

Most business contracts, especially founder's contracts, specify a legal jurisdiction. Legal jurisdiction designates the country or state legal system under which the company will operate. So, if a dispute arises, the judge or arbitrator will apply the laws of the legal jurisdiction to the proceedings. For instance, if a contract specifies California as the legal jurisdiction then California laws apply to the contract and will be interpreted with that in mind.

Different countries and states have different laws that will impact what founders can and can't do *regardless* of what they agree to in their contracts. For instance, California has certain minimum wage laws that are probably enforceable even if your contract specifies no cash payments (more on this below).

Most, but not all, of the country and state laws that impact founder's agreements pertain to employment and taxation.

Employment law covers minimum wages and ages, non-competition and whether a person should be treated as an employee or independent contractor—how a participant is categorized under the law could have a *major* impact on their rights and the company's obligations.

Tax law specifies how and when entities are taxed and the procedures for filing taxes. Depending on the circumstances, equity grants could be taxed as income or as capital gains (long or short term). Simply knowing how to file the right paperwork could have a *major* impact on how much tax you pay and when you pay it.

Because laws vary from country to country and from state to state, it is important to work with a lawyer who is familiar with your laws. You don't *have* to hire a lawyer to form a company, but without a lawyer you could overlook important details that could be costly down the road. A good start-up lawyer should be sensitive to cash restraints and help you get the most protection for your budget—they may even work for Pie!

Implementing Slicing Pie

In addition to all the legal issues above, you should take into account a number of other considerations when implementing the *Slicing Pie* model. Here are my high-level thoughts on the following:

1. *Slicing Pie* contracts
2. Local legal environment
3. Control
4. Minimizing taxes

Slicing Pie Contracts

Documenting the *Slicing Pie* method in a contract is fairly straightforward because the rules are clear and details on each rule are provided in *Slicing Pie* books. A good legal contract will include a description of both the allocation of slices and the recovery of slices.

Terms for Allocation

Your contract should include the following minimum terms for the allocation of equity:

- Slices or "units" (or whatever term you choose) should be calculated as follows:
  - Non-cash contributions are the *unpaid* portion of the fair market value of the contribution times the non-cash multiplier

- o Cash contributions are the amount of *unreimbursed* cash spent times the cash multiplier
- Upon termination of the *Slicing Pie* model equity or profit sharing will be allocated using the following calculation:
  - o Individual's slices ÷ all slices

Some lawyers may include more definition on fair market value and, of course, all the other legal stuff that is typically included in formation documents.

Terms for Recovery

The termination rules from *Slicing Pie* should be familiar to lawyers who have dealt with employment agreements as they are fairly standard language. Each separation definition from the recovery framework should be documented in the contract. In the event of termination, the terms covering the disposition of shares should include:

- Upon **termination for good reason** or **resignation for no good reason**
  - o Slices should be *recalculated* as follows:
    - Non-cash contributions, *except tangible property*, are the fair market value of the contribution times *zero*

- Cash contributions and the fair market value of tangible property are the amount of cash spent times *one*
  - The company may, at its own discretion, *force* a buyout at a price equal to the number of Slices times the model's currency ($1/Slice, for instance)
- Upon **termination for no good reason** or **resignation for good reason**
  - The company may, at its own discretion, *offer* a buyout at a price equal to the number of Slices times the model's currency ($1/Slice, for instance)

You may have chosen to include a time-based "Loyal Employee Clause" in the event of resignation with no good reason, as described in the chapter on recovery. If so, you will set a timeframe for the clause. Your contract should include a term like this:

- Upon resignation for no good reason
  - The company may, at its own discretion, *offer* a buyout at a price equal to the number of Slices contributed *before* _____ months times the model's currency ($1/Slice, for instance)

- Slices contributed *after* _____ months should be *recalculated* as follows:
  - Non-cash contributions, except tangible property, are the fair market value of the contribution times *zero*
  - Cash contributions and the fair market value of tangible property are the amount of cash spent times *one*
- The company may, at its own discretion, *force* a buyout at a price equal to the number of Slices times the model's currency ($1/Slice, for instance)

If your company has chosen to include a percentage-based "Loyal Employee Clause" in the event of resignation with no good reason, you will set a percentage retained for the clause. Your contract should include a term like this:

- Upon resignation for no good reason
  - The company may, at its own discretion, *offer* a buyout at a price equal to _____% times the number of slices times the model's currency ($1/Slice, for instance)
  - Remaining slices should be *recalculated* as follows:
    - Non-cash contributions, except tangible property, are the fair

> market value of the
> contribution times *zero*
- Cash contributions and the fair
  market value of tangible
  property are the amount of
  cash spent times *one*
  - The company may, at its own
    discretion, *force* a buyout at a price
    equal to the number of Slices times
    the model's currency ($1/Slice, for
    instance)

Local Legal Environment

In some cases, the rules outlined in *Slicing Pie* may run counter to local laws as mentioned above. For instance, the recovery framework recommends that when an employee is terminated with good reason or resigns for no good reason, they should agree to a non-compete agreement. There are many places where such agreements are *un*enforceable. This brings me to an important point: *there is a difference between legal rights and moral obligations*. In this case, just because a non-compete isn't enforceable, it doesn't mean it's fair to go out and compete. The *Slicing Pie* model *does not* recommend non-compete in the case of termination without cause or resignation with good cause. Remember, *Slicing Pie* is a moral agreement. If you are fired or quit for no reason, *don't* compete with the startup company you left, as it's not fair!

Contracts can be written in all sorts of ways that benefit one party over another. A savvy professional can easily take advantage of an inexperienced founder. I've seen all sorts of tricks. Just because a person agreed to an oppressive clause and just because it's legal does not mean that it's right. Beware of contracts that include language like this and even if your country or state won't enforce a fair contract term, don't think violating it is fair. A *Slicing Pie* contract should treat all parties with the same level of respect and fairness, and complying with the contract should be done in the spirit of the *Slicing Pie* model.

Here's another example: *Slicing Pie* calculates what's at risk based on the fair market value of the contributions made. At-risk implies that a person *might not get paid* for their contribution. Some places have minimum wage laws that make it *illegal* not to pay someone at least the minimum wage. In these cases, you would pay the minimum wage and subtract the payments from the fair market salary and reduce the contribution of Slices to the Pie accordingly. If your company can't afford to pay minimum wage you *will be in violation of the law*. You will have to discuss issues like this with your attorney and decide how you should handle them. In many cases, a departing employee may demand that you pay up!

Your lawyer will write a contract that reflects your local laws and customs, but please keep the spirit of *Slicing Pie* in mind when it comes to execution. Just because you have a legal right to act unfairly doesn't mean you should do it. If you have a legal *obligation*, on the other hand, you should always comply.

Control Issues

Slicing Pie will naturally give controlling interest to the person who has the most risk. This is logical and fair. I encourage decisions to be made with this in mind. Those who take the most risk should be able to steer the decisions in a direction they see fit. However, this may not always be a practical solution. In some cases, the person who takes the most risk may not even want control of the company.

Many people think they have to keep 51% of the equity in order to maintain control. While it is true that a 51% equity stake is a majority, it is not a good solution because 51% is a fixed amount and a fixed split is not fair. You don't have to take advantage of others to maintain control during the early days of your startup.

In the United States, LLCs can appoint managers who have decision-making powers regardless of their underlying ownership of the company. Terms can be written into contracts that designate control in any number of ways.

Profit sharing, rather than equity interests, can be used to provide financial benefits to Pie participants rather than control rights. Because many participants may be minority shareholders anyway, they may not care about their ability to cast a minority vote when it comes to important decisions. Different countries handle this in different ways.

Minimizing Taxes

Like my comments above, my comments below are intended to be a discussion guide for you and your lawyer or tax advisor. *I am not an attorney or a certified tax advisor.* Companies who use *Slicing Pie* are subject to the same taxes as companies who do not use *Slicing Pie*. The model will neither protect you from paying taxes, nor will it cause you to incur additional taxes. Just like any other business structure, you need to take the proper steps to ensure that you are filing the right kinds of documents with your country's revenue agency. The government deserves its fair share too! (But they won't take slices, unfortunately….)

This is where local knowledge of taxation really makes a difference. You should always act in a way that allows you to minimize taxes. There are all kinds of taxes, ranging from employment tax to income tax to capital gains tax.

In most jurisdictions, when shares are issued, income tax may be due on their underlying value. When shares are sold, capital gains may be due on the difference between what the owner paid (which could be nothing) and what the buyer paid.

It's important to keep in mind that the equity in a startup company rarely has any real value until it has either raised a Series A or it has generated meaningful, predictable revenue. Most of the time the *Slicing Pie* model will naturally "freeze" as described previously. At this point, the founders can terminate the model and move to a fixed split because personal risk is off the table and the model has delivered a perfectly fair split. The splits at different points along the way are less important because they don't lead to any financial gain (this isn't *always* true, but it's usually true).

The other thing to keep in mind is that taxation often occurs when equity is issued. The underlying value is often treated as income and the sale price is often treated as capital gains.

I've seen several approaches to minimizing tax and I'll cover two for the purposes of this handbook. Minimizing has to do with the timing and the value of the equity granted. Because the underlying value is usually $0, issuing equity early on rarely incurs tax (I've heard that some countries levy a tax regardless of value, however). The two basic approaches have a lot to do with the type of entity you choose. In the US the two most prominent structures are C-Corporation (C-Corp) and a Limited Liability Company (LLC).

Vesting

Usually used in a US-based C-Corp, restricted shares are issued at the outset of the company and

83(b) elections are filed by the recipients. The *Slicing Pie* model is used as a vesting schedule, where enough shares vest to keep the actual vested shares and the model in alignment.

For example, when an employee joins the company the company would issue a number of restricted shares subject to vesting according to *Slicing Pie*. You will want to use a number large enough so you won't run out - say, 10,000 shares. The recipient of the shares would be subject to income tax on the value of the shares, which is probably $0. Each period (month, day, week, whatever you choose), a number of shares would vest in order to bring it up to alignment with *Slicing Pie*.

Let's pretend Anson, Norvin and Merrily start a company with monthly vesting. They each get 10,000 restricted shares. At the end of the first month, *Slicing Pie* shows 33.3% each. Each person would vest *one* share. At the end of the next month the model shows Anson with 50% and Norvin and Merrily with 25%. Anson would vest one share more; the others would stay at one share each. Now Anson has two shares (50%) and Norvin and Merrily each have one (25%). The next month the model shows a 33.3% each split again. Norvin and Merrily each vest one more share. Anson vests nothing. Now each person has two shares or 33.3% each. This continues until the Pie terminates, at which point all unvested shares return to the company or are bought back by the company at a nominal cost. In later months you may have to vest dozens or hundreds of shares to bring people into alignment.

Traditional Vesting

Traditional vesting is time-based and is intended to protect companies from the problems caused by fixed equity splits. It allows companies to enter into a fixed split agreement, but maintain some recourse in case someone leaves or doesn't work out. By implementing a vesting schedule, the company can remove an employee before their shares have vested. Or, if a person leaves they would forfeit the unvested portion of their shares. Vesting schedules are better than no vesting schedules, but they cause problems. For instance, an unscrupulous employer can fire employees *before* they vest and keep their shares. Or, an unscrupulous employee can quit the day *after* their shares vest. This kind of thing happens all the time (I've seen it) and it's perfectly legal, but that doesn't mean it's fair. The *Slicing Pie* model is a much better way.

Buy-Backs

A buy-back allows a company to buy shares back from a participant at a pre-determined price in order to bring them into alignment with the *Slicing Pie* model. The price is usually set based on the value at the time the stock is issued. For most startups it will be nominal. This can help minimize tax upon termination of the model.

Suited for C-Corps or LLCs, each person would be granted a fixed, restricted membership interest at the outset of the venture. Upon termination, the company would *buy back* interest from some of the participants based on *Slicing Pie*.

For example, Anson and Norvin start an LLC and take a 50% membership interest each. Upon termination, *Slicing Pie* shows a 60/40 split. The company would buy back membership interest from Norvin at a nominal price until his share was 40%, leaving Anson with 60%.

You can download a buy-back spreadsheet to help you do the math at www.SlicingPie.com.

Profit Sharing

As mentioned before, the *Slicing Pie* model can be used to dictate the distribution of profits or proceeds from a sale, regardless of the underlying ownership structure. I personally like the profit sharing option because it saves a lot of legal and tax headaches. In fact, I often recommend using profit sharing rather than actual equity. If you issue equity, you have to jump through a lot more legal hoops than you would if you use profit sharing. For instance, adding a new member to your LLC might require an amendment to your operating agreement that would require signatures from all the other members. How much time do you want to spend preparing this paperwork and chasing people down for signatures?

Don't Cheat!

Whether you like it or not, the government is on your startup team. It provides the legal and economic framework—good or bad—in which your company exists. They, like you, deserve their fair share. **Do not try to evade taxes**. Pay what you owe, but not *more* than you owe.

Intellectual Property

In some cases, a person will transfer ownership or otherwise assign intellectual property rights to a startup. Depending on the nature of the transfer, it may have legal *and* tax implications. If your company requires the transfer of intellectual property, I *highly* recommend you find someone familiar with the rules in your country.

Next Steps

For attorneys with clients wishing to implement a *Slicing Pie* model, there is help available through SlicingPie.com. Please contact me; I am happy to provide anything you need to properly implement a *Slicing Pie* model for your client.

I'm in the process of working with attorneys in other countries to create localized guidelines. Links to these sites will be available on SlicingPie.com.

If you *are* an attorney and would like to become your country's local expert, please let me know!

Summary

This chapter is intended to get you on the right path, it is not supposed to be a comprehensive guide to legal issues facing startups, nor is it intended to replace actual professional advice from attorneys and accountants.

The *Slicing Pie* model is a new way of allocating equity or profit sharing in a startup company. It provides a much fairer method than anything currently available, but because it is new, it may be met with some skepticism. The best implementations adhere closely to the recommendations in the book so the model can do what it is designed to do. When changes are made, it becomes more likely that traditional disputes will arise.

Most business lawyers and accountants are well-versed in traditional equity structures, but they may not have exposure to the *Slicing Pie* model. Do not let this deter you from achieving fairness in your company. The *Slicing Pie* model can easily be documented for legal and tax issues. Visit SlicingPie.com for help finding a lawyer that can help you get the right agreements in place for you and your team.

Additional Reading

Slicing Pie-friendly lawyers are people who understand the value of dynamic equity models and are familiar with the mechanics of the *Slicing Pie* model. We list some of them on our website. Visit the link below to find some lawyers and get access to *Slicing Pie* legal agreement templates.

www.slicingpie.com/silcing-pie-friendly-lawyers

Chapter Eleven:

Retrofit/Forecast

Many founders discover the *Slicing Pie* model *after* they have already succumbed to a dreaded fixed split. This chapter outlines the process for *retrofitting* the *Slicing Pie* model using the **Retrofitting/Forecast Tool** spreadsheet that you can download at:

www.SlicingPie.com/retrofit-forecast

The *first* step is to get everyone on board with the *Slicing Pie* model. You may need to loan them a copy of this book or buy them their own copy. Skeptics can read the chapter called, "Convincing Prospects" first. You can get discounted six-packs on SlicingPie.com.

The *next* step is to go back in time and remember everything that everyone did since you started the company. This is harder than it sounds, but as long as you do your best you're probably going to be okay. Use the *Slicing Pie*

Retrofit/Forecast Tool to record your recreation of the past.

Forecasting

The tool can also be used to *forecast* the split after a certain period of time. To forecast, you will record your *guesses* about the future rather than your recollection of the past.

Don't rely too much on a forecast as it's much harder to predict the future than it is to remember the past. However, people may want to know how their participation can translate into equity, so this exercise can be comforting. Keep in mind, however, that things rarely go as planned.

The Spreadsheet

The retrofit/forecast tool takes a *single* snapshot in time. The results of this exercise should be the *starting* point for the tracking spreadsheets or online Pie Slicer software available at SlicingPie.com.

This tool is not for tracking contributions over time. For that, use the Pie Slicer software or the tracking spreadsheet.

Editing

The spreadsheet has a mix of user-entered fields and calculated fields. Enter data where indicated by a box, but please don't monkey around with the formulas.

Pie Settings

At the top of the spreadsheet is a settings box that is pre-filled to reflect the rules in this book and the *Slicing Pie* book and I *don't* recommend changing the multipliers or the hours in a year, but you can update the commission and finder's fee to reflect your company's policy.

Grunt Fund Settings

Cash Multiplier	Non-Cash Multiplier	Sales Commission	Investor Finder Fee	Hours in a Year
4	2	10%	5.00%	2000

There is only one Investor Finder's Fee level which is set to the recommended rate for fund raises under $1,000,000. I did this to simplify the spreadsheet, reasoning that companies who have raised more than $1,000,000 may not need the *Slicing Pie* model. Details on finder's fees are covered in an earlier chapter.

Date Settings

Set the date of the retrofit in the Date of Retrofit/Forecast box. In the case of a Forecast, you would want to set a future date.

Date of Retrofit/ Forecast
24-Jun-15

"Date Work Began in Earnest" is the first date the individual began working on the project with the intent of becoming part of the team. In some cases, casual contributors may not have made any real commitment to the project and may not be included. The spreadsheet uses the date settings to estimate the amount of time contributed by each person.

Contributions

Calculations for contributions are made according to the rules in this book and the *Slicing Pie* book. If you are familiar with the model, the entries should be fairly straightforward.

Remember that *Slicing Pie* allocates equity based on the relative amount of risk taken by each person. The amount of risk taken is equal to whatever a person would have been paid by someone else for the same contribution. *Slicing Pie* also applies a risk multiplier/normalizer that rewards individuals for taking the risk and normalizes cash and non-cash contributions.

Fair Market Salary

In many cases, founders who have entered into a fixed-split model have *not* discussed salary at all. Knowing a person's salary, even if you don't pay them, is important because it allows you to measure what they are putting at risk.

Remember, the fair market salary is the salary the employee would be paid by an established company, for *similar* work and is the agreed-upon salary for the position that *will be paid* as soon as the company is *able* to pay. In other words, negotiate this as if you are going to pay it, because someday you will (hopefully).

The number will fall in the intersection of the company's willingness to pay and the employee's willingness to accept the pay.

Make sure the salaries you pay reflect the reality of the job you are hiring for. A startup (you) may not need a full-time senior-level VP of marketing who can get $300,000 a year on the open market. People like this usually manage big teams, big budgets and have big responsibilities. You may want a more junior-level marketing guy with half the salary. A $300,000-a-year marketing VP may not want a startup job with a fair market salary of $150,000 per year unless they believe the value of the company will grow quickly, in which case the pay cut might be worth it.

Similarly, avoid the temptation to pay "start-up rates" which are lower than fair market rate. Set the salary at what the job is worth.

The spreadsheet will determine an hourly rate based on the number of hours in the settings area. The default is 2,000 which assumes 40 hours per week and 50 weeks a year. Yes, I know there are 52 weeks in a year, but even entrepreneurs need a couple of weeks of vacation! Some countries have different hours in a working week.

Average Hours per Week Worked

It's difficult to determine *exactly* how many hours a person worked unless they kept good records. Estimate the hours worked on a regular basis. Keep in mind that if you claim you worked huge hours (60+) *before* the retrofit and don't continue to work that much *after* the retrofit, your teammates may think you are untrustworthy. Similarly, if you log lots of hours, but *don't* show corresponding productivity you may damage your credibility. I recommend you err on the side of underestimating, rather than overestimating.

Going forward you and your team will track your time contributions in as much detail as you feel comfortable.

Cash

Minor working capital is money deposited into a corporate checking account for the purposes of paying bills.

Expenses are business-related costs incurred by an individual. Personal living expenses do not count.

Only include money that was spent on business expenses. The *Slicing Pie* model accounts for cash consumed, not cash invested.

Equipment and Supplies

Equipment and supplies bought for the company are treated as cash. Use the price paid, or estimate the price if receipts aren't available. (In the future, keep receipts!) Be careful not to double-count items that may have been included in entries for cash.

For items less than a year old, the purchase price is treated as a non-cash contribution because it was not a current expense incurred on behalf of the company.

For items older than a year use the resale value. Check eBay or Craigslist to help estimate value.

Facilities

Enter the fair rent for the space used.

Intellectual Property

There are two sections for intellectual property. Both should be used in situations where the intellectual property was developed *prior* to the person starting or joining the company. Intellectual property developed while on the job is simply part of the job and would not necessarily receive special treatment.

In some cases, the company may want to use the time & expenses related to the development of the intellectual property. This would be common for a solo founder who creates the IP *before* the company starts.

In other cases, the company may want to use a royalty model. This would be common for a company that *acquires* IP after the company has started. There is a field for an advance. In the licensing world, advances are common. This gives the inventor a stake in the company even if the company fails to move on the idea. Without an advance, companies would have an incentive to license technology without any intent to commercialize it simply to keep it off the market. That wouldn't be fair. Advances are standard practice, but the amount of the advance is deducted from future royalties.

Commissions & Investor Relations

A person's relationships translate into value if they generate revenue or investment. Enter the amount generated. The rate is set for all participants in the settings area. Usually, commissions apply only to commissioned salespeople because they would have a lower base salary.

Forgone

In some cases, the spreadsheet will calculate a "Forgone" sum. This is simply reiterating that payments may not have been paid. I don't want to imply that anyone is necessarily owed a sum.

You don't need to "net-out" entries in the spreadsheet. Rather, you just need to enter what was contributed. As you will see below, the tool will adjust the amounts in the event that payments were made to individuals.

Adjustments

Lower on the spreadsheet there is a space for cash payments made to individuals. It does not necessarily matter what the payment was for. It only matters that it was made.

Payments from the company to an individual will lower their at-risk taken contributions.

Payments will be treated as the repayment of cash first, because with the default multiplier (4), cash translates into more slices than non-cash. In the *Slicing Pie* model cash is more "expensive" in terms of slices than non-cash.

After cash payments are deducted from cash contributions the remainder will apply to non-cash contributions.

Overcompensation

Sometimes, after adjusting the contributions with cash payments, a person has a *zero* balance. This means they have not risked anything and, therefore, would not have slices.

In the event the balance is negative, you are dealing with someone who has been *over*compensated and no slices will be allocated. The model will not allocate negative slices. Be careful not to overpay people in the future!

Bonus Slices

In some cases, it may be appropriate to provide a spot bonus in slices to a deserving team member in the case of exceptional work or contribution that wouldn't otherwise warrant an increase in fair market salary.

Interpreting the Retrofit

After all the contributions have been accounted for, you can compare the *Slicing Pie* allocation to the fixed split allocation. They probably will not match. The degree to which they don't match may cause some discomfort among the team members.

For instance, the *Slicing Pie* model might allocate a much lower share to a person who had a large share under the fixed model. They may be upset. Hopefully, they will see that they had an unfair allocation and will realize that the new allocation better reflects their contribution relative to the other members of the team. They can take comfort in knowing that they are being fair and the team will get along better using the new model.

In some cases, the individual will hem and haw and not budge. This means they do not fully understand the *Slicing Pie* model and its ability to be fair.

Or, if they *do* understand the model, it means that they are the kind of person who is quite willing to benefit at the expense of others. The world is full of people like this and I'm sorry you have one on your team. This may doom your company. If this happens to you, let me know and I'll try to walk you through a strategy for dealing with this.

Moving Forward

Once you and your team agree to the retrofit, you can simply transfer the results to the *Slicing Pie* tracking spreadsheet.

If you are using the online Pie Slicer software, simply enter each team member's adjusted cash and non-cash contribution using the "Other" contribution type from the dropdown menu:

You will have to enter each amount separately, being careful to select the appropriate "Cash" or "Non-Cash" radio button:

Summary

The retrofitting exercise should be a frank and open discussion about the contributions each person has made. It should not be confrontational, but it may make people uncomfortable. However, it's not nearly as uncomfortable as sitting in a courtroom suing your former friends and colleagues over an equity disagreement. This happens all the time, but not to you!

Chapter Thirteen:

Objections

Slicing Pie is a new way of thinking about very old problem. Many smart people suffer from fear of the new (Neophobia) and fear of change (Metathesiophobia). *Slicing Pie* requires people to not only consider something new, but also change the way they think about a problem that's been around since the Paleolithic era when cave men carved bad equity agreements in stone (I think).

Traditional splits, as flawed as they are, feel safe and snuggly to people who know how to work with them. Faced with *Slicing Pie*, these people will furl their brows, cross their arms, and begin to squirm in their seats. I've seen it all.

I've been facing *Slicing Pie* naysayers for years and I've become more adept at responding to them. If you or your partners are feeling skeptical about the model, below are some of the more common objections I've heard over the years and my attempt to address them. In my experience, objections are *good* things. Someone who raises objections is someone who is thinking through the model and trying to understand it. Once someone gets their head around the model they are more likely to object to traditional models rather than *Slicing Pie*. Many skeptics turn into fans.

Slicing Pie works. I've never found an equity problem that *Slicing Pie* won't improve. *Every bootstrapped startup in the world should use Slicing Pie!*

My Partners Don't Want to Use It

In my experience, there are three main reasons why someone would not want to use *Slicing Pie*.

The *first* reason is that they don't fully understand how it works and why it's fair. If this is the case, ask them to access the books, videos, games and articles on the subject or even set up a call with me. Education is the first step.

The *second* reason is that they understand it, but don't want to keep track of their contributions. The *Slicing Pie* software makes this really easy. It takes minimal effort. So little effort, in fact, that if it's still a deal breaker for them, they may not be the kind of person who can get stuff done.

The *third* reason is that they are the kind of person who is willing to benefit from an unfair split. *Do not* work with these people.

I Want to Maintain Control

Slicing Pie will give control the person with the most at risk. This is how it should be. The person with the most to lose should be able to exert control over major decisions. It's not really fair for someone with less at risk to exclude someone with more at risk. So, if you want to maintain control, be the person who contributes the most.

That being said, there are reasons why consolidating control to one person or group of people may be a necessity. The good news is that there are a number of structures that would allow consolidated control even—for a minority shareholder—while still providing fair financial benefits to other shareholders:

- A *Slicing Pie* profit-sharing program would provide all the financial benefits to partners while consolidating control to select individuals.

- A *Slicing Pie* vesting or buyback program can be set up to consolidate decision making to select individuals for a period of time.

Control is *not* a reason to implement an unfair split.

It's Too Complicated, I Want Something Simple

Like many things in life, *Slicing Pie* is more complex than just guessing (which is how most equity splits are created). But, the basic principle *is* quite simple:

A person's % share of the rewards should always equal that person's % share of what's put at risk to achieve those rewards.

The simplicity of *Slicing Pie* is what makes it work. Yes, you have to understand how to determine fair market value and yes, you have to keep track of what people are doing and how money is spent; but these are basic skills of any good business person. Real complexity comes in the form of legal disputes over fixed equity splits that always seem to come to a head when you're trying to raise money or grow your company.

My Lawyer Said There Will Be Legal and Tax Issues

Of course there will be! *Every* company faces legal and tax issues no matter how it's structured. *Slicing Pie* companies face the *exact same* issues and, like with any corporate structure, the issues need to be addressed.

Your lawyer may not have experience with *Slicing Pie* so it's easier for them to steer you in a direction they are more familiar with, but that doesn't mean there's something wrong with *Slicing Pie*. It simply means your lawyer doesn't want to learn about something new. Tell your lawyer that *Slicing Pie* has been successfully implemented all over the world and that I will *personally* spend some time with them to bring them up to speed on how it works. If they still don't like it, find a new lawyer.

There's Too Much Uncertainty

Some people think that dividing up equity in fixed chunks provides more certainty than a dynamic program like *Slicing Pie*. That is a misconception. The truth is that *all* equity splits are dynamic because they *all* change. No matter what founders do with their split in the beginning it's bound to change as the mix of team members and investors and partners change (as is *always* the case). *Slicing Pie* simply gives you a fair, logical, automated way of managing this change. The alternative is to constantly renegotiate the fixed split. That's why I call it the "Fix & Fight" model.

Nobody Likes Tracking Their Time

Me neither! Tracking time is kind of a hassle, but you and your team can determine how much granularity you want to track. You can track by hour or day or week or month or even year!

The increments need to be useful enough to capture differences in commitment. If you're tracking by day, for instance, a person working one hour per day is clearly not as committed as a person working 14 hours a day. If your whole team is working full time if may be less of an issue than a team with different levels of commitment.

Once people understand that their equity level depends in part on their level of time commitment, tracking becomes less of an issue. Additionally, good time records are an invaluable tool for managing employees and investor due diligence. Imagine being able to show a potential investor detailed records of how your company developed, who did what and how you spent money—it's an incredible tool.

Productivity is More Important Than Hours On the Job

I agree, but most jobs in the non-startup world pay people for based on time, not on productivity.

Imagine being in a job where each week your manager would assess your productivity and only pay you what she thought you were worth that week. It would be an insane nightmare.

Slicing Pie reflects reality. In the non-startup world, people are expected to perform and are paid on a regular basis based on the expected performance. Really productive employees get bonuses or raises and unproductive get fired.

Some jobs are easy to tie to productivity. Sales or piecework, for instance, can be paid for performance. If your work is highly variable this is much harder and often impractical.

It's Too Much Work

Tracking inputs does take a little discipline, but all good businesses require discipline. *Slicing Pie* sits on top of things most good businesses do anyway.

Most business track sales, investments, commissions and expenses anyway. Most people are comfortable with saving receipts and keeping track of out-of-pocket business expenses. Most people can manage their personal schedule and are in-tune with how they spend their time. If someone on your team thinks these things sound like too much work, maybe you should reconsider their participation.

Investors Won't Like It

Professional investors want a clean, fair, logical, conflict-free cap table which is exactly what *Slicing Pie* delivers. It also delivers records of who is doing what and how money is spent- pure gold during due diligence.

Traditional fixed splits tend to create disgruntled absentee owners, team member disputes and complex cap-tables with multiple classes of stock and poorly-negotiated shareholder's agreements. Investors *definitely* won't like that!

My Advisors Told Me to Stick with Traditional Approaches

If you're advisors are telling you this, they don't understand the model. Get them up to speed by sharing this book, pointing them to SlicingPie.com or connecting them with me personally. Business is constantly in flux and a good advisor should be informed on best practices. *Slicing Pie* is a significant improvement over traditional models. If your advisor doesn't appreciate the model, please find a new advisor, or don't take their advice and use *Slicing Pie* anyway.

Other Objections?

If you, or your teammates, partners, employees, lawyers, accountants, advisors, investors, suppliers, professors, mothers, fathers, sisters, brothers, uncles, aunts and drinking buddies have other objections please, please, *please* contact me at **Mike@SlicingPie.com**.

If you are bootstrapping your startup, Slicing Pie *will* work for you, I promise. Do *not* split your equity another way, you will only be setting yourself up for failure!

Chapter Fourteen:

Resources

As far as I know, you are holding in your hands a description of the only equity model on the planet that isn't based primarily on wild guesses about the future, rules of thumb and negotiation skills. Many of the people who provide traditional equity advice are incredibly smart, well-intentioned and have plenty of good experience. But they may lack a model, like the *Slicing Pie* model, that is based on observable values with mechanisms for maintaining fairness in spite of what changes. I believe that if they take a serious look at the *Slicing Pie* model they will see the value and never go back to their old ways. This will create a better environment for entrepreneurs everywhere.

 I spend time on *Slicing Pie* every day, even on vacation. I'm constantly writing, speaking and teaching whenever I get the chance (let me know if you would like me to speak at your company or organization). I want the model to be as accessible as possible and I want to do everything I can to provide the tools people need to understand how it works. Below are a few resources that are available:

Slicing Pie: *Funding Your Company Without Funds*

Slicing Pie is the first book I wrote on this subject and I consider it the definitive guide on fair equity splits. It is available at Amazon.com in print, Kindle and audiobook. It can be ordered through most bookstores. You can buy six-packs at www.slicingpie.com/sixers. The book is available in a number of other languages and additional translations are in the works!

A La Mode/Resources

A section of SlicingPie.com contains letter templates, cheat sheets and case studies to supplement the book *Slicing Pie.* Content includes:

Slicing Pie Lawyers

Several attorneys have created template agreements for the *Slicing Pie* model. These templates are available for purchase and come with free consultations. Visit:

www.slicingpie.com/silcing-pie-friendly-lawyers

Tracking Tools

Besides the Pie Slicer tool described in this book, I also have an Excel spreadsheet you can download. Some people have posted Google Docs and Apple Numbers spreadsheets too. To download the spreadsheet visit:

www.slicingpie.com/the-grunt-fund-calculator

Videos

I post videos of lectures, seminars and tools on YouTube and on SlicingPie.com.

Blog

I regularly post updates to my blog responding to reader questions or providing additional clarification on the model.

Workshops & Seminars

You can attend live in-person or online workshops & seminars about the *Slicing Pie* model. I've been all over the world. I post events open to the public at: **www.slicingpie.com/events**

If you are part of an organization that would be interested in sponsoring a live event please let me know. More information is available at: **www.slicingpie.com/book-mike-to-speak**

Games

I've developed two games that help people better understand the benefits of the *Slicing Pie* model and get comfortable with the mechanics of how they work. Both are free.

The Slicing Pie Board Game

Available at **www.slicingpie.com/game**, the game simulates the life cycle of a startup company. It requires you to print out a game board and game cards and find some dice and playing pieces (I use Legos), so it's a little impractical for casual users, but I use it in the classes I teach and students love it.

The Slicing Pie eCard Game

Based on the board game, this game also simulates the life cycle of a startup. All the components of the game are available online, so it's easier to access and play. I use it for larger events and remote events. You can find everything you need at **www.slicingpie.com/slicing-pie-card-game**.

International Resources

I'm working with individuals in other countries to bring *Slicing Pie* to international audiences. These people have helped with translations, created meetup   groups   and   identified   local   legal assistance.

Talk to Mike

I do my best to make myself available. You can schedule   live   calls   with   me   on **www.slicingpie.com/about-mike**. Please feel free to reach out to me with any questions, comments, or concerns.

Clarity:	clarity.fm/mikemoyer
Email:	Mike@SlicingPie.com
Twitter:	@GruntFunds/@MikeMoyer
Facebook:	facebook.com/mikedmoyer
LinkedIn:	linkedin.com/in/mikemoyer
Website:	SlicingPie.com
	MikeMoyer.com

I look forward to working with you and I wish you the very best of luck with your startup!

Chapter Fifteen:

The Pie Slicer

The online Pie Slicer is a web-based application that allows founders to track contributions and equity allocations for their team. It was developed because lots of people said, "You should create a tracking program." In fact, several people have independently launched similar programs based on the *Slicing Pie* model. However, these programs may or may not reflect the actual calculations in my books and I wanted readers to have an application that is true to the model.

The rules and logic built into the Pie Slicer application are *exactly* as described in this book. This includes both the allocation framework and the recovery framework. The calculations will also mirror the Excel spreadsheet. But, the spreadsheet has limitations that the software does not. After all, it's a spreadsheet and not a software program.

I recommend using the model as described here, as any modifications are bound to make the model less fair.

However, some people choose to use a modified version of the *Slicing Pie* model. If you are someone who has chosen to modify the model, the Excel spreadsheet is probably the best place to start because you can make your own modifications.

If you want to use the model as outlined in this book the Pie Slicer application will work nicely. You can still modify a few things in the Pie Settings screen.

Using the Pie Slicer

Like most online applications, the Pie Slicer is designed to be intuitive and self-explanatory. Help text is built into the program and we will continue to upgrade and enhance the program based on user feedback. It is an easy program to use.

However, without a base understanding of how dynamic equity splits work, the tool may not be fully adopted by the team. I wrote this book to help shed light on the interworking of the model and the importance of dynamic equity splits such as the *Slicing Pie* model. My intent, however, is that you can enjoy this book and make use of its contents, whether or not you use the Pie Slicer application.

Display

The Home tab in the Pie Slicer is the main display page. It tells you just about everything you need to know about your Pie. On the left are the members of your team, default images are "Grunts," which are fictional animals I created to represent a hard-working startup employee.

A Grunt

On the right is a pie chart showing the current split and a bar chart showing Well balances for each participant.

At the top you will see the number of slices in the Pie and the total amount of money in the Well.

User Roles

There are four primary user roles in the application: Pie owner, employee, executive and advisor. The Pie owner creates the Pie on their account and pays the monthly or annual fee. Only owners have "all access" to the tool with the ability to view and edit all the settings, including salaries and Pie settings.

Only Pie owners can log contributions from *all* members in addition to their own, and only they can make deposits and withdrawals from the Well. This ensures there is one point of contact for the Pie.

Pie owners can add new members to the team. When a new member is added, they will receive and email inviting them to join the Pie and input their own contributions. When users are added you can designate them as Executives, Employees or Advisors.

🕸 Pie Slicer

To add a team member, click the "Add Team Member" button in the upper left side of the screen.

Individuals have control over how their names and avatars appear on the site so you will not be able to edit their name or avatar after you add them.

Members of the team can log their own contributions through their own account. However, even if they don't set up their account, you can add contributions for them.

Executives have the same *view* into the Pie as the Pie owner, but they will not be able to change the settings for anything except a few personal settings. *Only* Pie owners have the ability to change all the settings.

Employees and Advisors cannot view any information related to the Pie, except for their personal contributions. The main difference between an Employee and an Advisor is that the Advisor can't be fired as described earlier.

Below are screenshots of the same Pie as viewed from the point of view of different account types. Notice that in the Advisor and Employee view the other team members do *not* appear and that the buttons are grayed-out for adding team members and managing the Well. This person's access is limited to their own activities.

Pie Owner & Executive View

Employee & Advisor View

Logging Contributions

The *Slicing Pie* model requires people to track their contributions of expenses, equipment, ideas, supplies, facilities, sales and, most importantly, time. The Pie Slicer includes tracking for all contributions so it can properly allocate slices based on an individual's contributions. This can be done as often as you and your team sees fit. Individuals can sign in and log their contributions at their convenience, or the Pie owner can do it for them. The Pie Slicer keeps track of all the contributions and when people last logged in so the Pie owner can provide a gentle reminder when necessary.

Many people cringe when asked to keep track of their time. They usually don't mind tracking their *expenses*, but they don't like tracking their time. You and your team can decide the level of granularity you will track using the Pie Slicer and the detail of the notes captured, but I don't recommend trying to avoid this task altogether. Understanding how you and your team spend your time is as important as keeping track of your expenses (maybe even *more* important).

The time-tracking tools in the Pie Slicer are basic and will allow your team to input their time, allocate the time to a specific project or category, and provide a description of what they did during that chunk of time. We tried to make it as painless as possible. We don't like tracking our time either!

 **Pie Slicer**

The Pie Slicer has some default projects built in. You can delete these and/or add your own. Under the settings menu, click on Pie Settings.

Multiple Pies

A user can participate in multiple Pies at one time. They can be invited to participate as an individual contributor or they can start their own Pie. The active Pie's name will appear in the upper left side of the screen. Click the name to change Pies or start a new one. Pie owners have control over the Pie settings, can add users, and are responsible for the payment. Thank you, by the way, for your payment!

Individuals have control over their own information such as name and image, but only Pie owners can set the salary. Salaries are set per Pie depending on what your role is. If you are the VP of marketing for one Pie and the burger-flipper for another, your VP role will probably have a higher fair market salary.

Tabs

The tabs across the top provide the following functionality:

Home	Brings the user to the main page with the Pie chart.

Reports	Access a variety of reports like your current cap table, a list of contributions and some other analytics
Account	Access to the variables that can be changed by the individual account owner.
Help	Tips and information about the tool. Access to Customer Service.

Settings

The Pie Slicer has a variety of settings that impact how slices are calculated. Most of the settings are pretty self-explanatory, but I will cover a few critical settings here.

Team Member Settings

Pie owners can invite team members by email and name. If the person is already in the Pie Slicer database (by email), the existing name and image will supersede the name entered when adding the individual. Individuals have control over their own name and image if they don't want to keep the default Grunt avatar mentioned earlier.

Once the individual contributor is added to the Pie, they can log contributions. The Pie owner can also log contributions on their behalf. After a team member is added, the Pie Owner can still edit their settings by clicking on the little gear icon found above and to the right of the team member's avatar.

Salary is required when adding the team member for the first time. When entering salary, input the fair market salary *less* whatever cash compensation is being paid from the company account. If you start paying more, you should edit this field. The Pie Slicer will automatically convert the salary to an hourly rate by dividing by 2,000, which is roughly the number of working hours in a year for a full-time job. In the U.S. a full-time job is 40 hours per week and most Americans take two weeks off for vacation. Most countries have a similar number, although vacation time varies. As long as all the participants are using the same calculation for hourly rate, there is no need to adjust this number.

If the Pie owner edits a team member's salary, the change will only affect *future* calculations; it will *not* go back in time and change past contributions. This is true for all changes made to settings.

Pie Settings

To access Pie Settings, click the Pie Setting button above the team members. The Pie settings screen is where you set the parameters used in the calculations for your Pie. Below is a description of the impact the settings will make on your Pie. Changes to any of the settings will only affect future contributions; they will not affect past contributions.

Currency	Use the primary currency that your company operates under. When calculating a buyout, a slice will be converted into that currency on a 1:1 basis. The Pie Slicer will not consider exchange rates. Please note that buyout price is *not* the same thing as value. It is simply the fair price to pay someone to get their slices back when they leave.
Non-Cash Multiplier	This is the multiplier for non-cash contributions including pre-owned equipment and supplies. The default setting is 2. I don't recommend changing this for reasons described earlier.
Cash Multiplier	This is the multiplier for cash contributions including equipment and supplies purchased for the company, unreimbursed expenses and cash. The default setting is 4. I don't recommend changing this for reasons described earlier.

Commission Rate	This is the rate (%) used to calculate commission on revenue generated by commissioned salespeople. Not everyone will be entitled to a commission. Set the rate based on fair market rates for your industry. This can vary dramatically, so you'll need to do a little research to get the right number. The default is 10%.
Royalty Rate	This is the rate (%) used to calculate royalty payable to the owners of intellectual property behind the ideas that generate revenue. Set the rate based on fair market rates for your industry. This can vary dramatically, so you'll need to do a little research to get the right number. The default is 5%.
Finder's Fee	If your company wants to award a finder's fee to people who bring in investments (not common), you can set two rates. One for the first X amount of cash, and one for the rest of the cash.

Personal Car	Your company can decide how it wants to calculate slices when people use their own cars for work.
Projects	Projects are used to see how time and resources are being spent. You can add or subtract projects.
Reset Pie	Resetting the Pie will erase all transactions so you can start over.
Delete Pie	Deleting the Pie will erase all your data and terminate payments.

Be sure to click "Save Changes" when you make changes!

By the way, technology changes faster than books so there may be slightly different options online. Rest assured, the underlying *Slicing Pie* model will not change, however.

Calculations

The Pie Slicer will convert contributions to slices using the calculations described in this book. Below is a summary of these calculations:

Contribution	Calculation
Time	((Fair Market Salary ÷ 2000) x Hours) x Non Cash Multiplier
Expenses	(Amount Paid – Reimbursed) x Cash Multiplier
Supplies → New	(Amount Paid – Reimbursed) x Cash Multiplier
Supplies → Less Than a Year Old	(Amount Paid – Reimbursed) x **Non**-Cash Multiplier
Supplies → Older Than a Year	(Fair Market Value – Reimbursed) x **Non**-Cash Multiplier
Equipment → New	(Amount Paid – Reimbursed) x Cash Multiplier
Equipment → Less Than a Year Old	(Amount Paid – Reimbursed) x **Non**-Cash Multiplier
Equipment → Older Than a Year	(Fair Market Value – Reimbursed) x **Non**-Cash Multiplier
Sales	((Sale Amount x Royalty) – Cash Payment) x Non Cash multiplier
Finder's Fee	((Amount Raised < Cut Off x Pre-Cut Off %) + ((Amount Raised > Cut Off x Post Cut-Off %)
Facilities	(Fair Market Value – Cash Payment) x Non-Cash multiplier
Other	Amount x Cash multiplier OR Non-Cash multiplier (depending on choice)

Personal Car	(Fair Market Value – Reimbursed) x Chosen Multiplier OR (Fuel Cost – Reimbursed) x Cash Multiplier PLUS (((Miles or Kilometers x Flat Rate) – Fuel Costs)) – Reimbursed Remainder) x Non-Cash Multiplier

The Well

The Well works as described above in the Cash Contributions chapter. Slices are allocated to individuals based on their ownership of the Well at the time the money was withdrawn, not when it's deposited.

When adding funds to the Well, the Pie Slicer will apply the Finder's Fee calculation only if an individual is named as the Finder's Fee Recipient.

Summary

If you are familiar with the *Slicing Pie* model as described in this book, the Pie Slicer should be fairly self-explanatory. The tool is designed to track contributions and apply the allocation and recovery calculations as described.

Pie owners have control over who is a member of the team, what information they can see and the settings that drive the calculations. The default settings are the recommended settings.

About the Author

Mike Moyer is a professional entrepreneur who has started companies from scratch, joined start-up companies, helped others start companies, raised millions of dollars of start-up capital, and helped sell start-up companies.

He has worked in a variety of industries ranging from vacuum cleaners and motor home chassis to fine wine.

Mike has a MS in Integrated Marketing Communication from Northwestern University and an MBA from the University of Chicago. He teaches Entrepreneurship at both universities. Mike lives in Lake Forest, Illinois, with his wife and three kids, and the Lizard of Oz.

Other Books by Mike Moyer:

- **Slicing Pie**- the original book on dynamic splits
- **Pitch Ninja**- about giving an awesome presentation
- **Trade Show Samurai**- how to capture lots and lots of leads at your next show

Mike is also the author of *Get Them Gators, How to Make Colleges Want You, Perfect Parent Hats, and Business Basics*

Appendix

Changes from Original Slicing Pie Model

I never anticipated the positive impact that my first book on this subject, *Slicing Pie*, would have on entrepreneurs who previously struggled with how to divide up equity in their startup company. I have been flattered by the positive feedback I've received from readers, and I've enjoyed meeting them at *Slicing Pie* events all over the world.

Most importantly, however, I've learned more about how the model works for them and how I can help them implement it in their companies. I keep track of feedback, and I try to incorporate it into articles I write, speeches I give, and new versions of the book. Although the basic model has not changed, I have tried to clarify or add detail to the best way to implement it.

This book, the *Slicing Pie Handbook*, is intended to be a practical guide for teams implementing the model based on the best practices I have learned from actual users. The model described in this book is the *same* model described in *Slicing Pie*; it's just a more updated explanation with more depth in certain areas. If you want more back story on the development of the model or further commentary on why I designed it the way I did, you should read *Slicing Pie*. Or, if you want to read some case studies on implementation, read *Slicing Pie*. You can read this book or that book or both books. The books are intended to reinforce and complement each other.

Changes

The *Slicing Pie* model was developed over a number of years based on my personal research as well as my own trial and error. I tweaked the model until I was comfortable with it and then published the first version of the book in October 2012. Since then, updates haven't changed the core model, but I have tried to clarify and add more depth to how the model is understood. However, this book contains a few minor changes to the original model that are worth noting. The changes apply to the description in this book and the online Pie Slicer. The following elements are different than described in *Slicing Pie* version 2.3 and earlier:

Grunt Funds

If you have already read my other books on this subject, you will notice that I don't refer to the model as a "Grunt Fund" in this book. That is because the term is difficult to translate into other languages. One translator suggested the translation, "Pig Money," which doesn't work, so I'm writing for a more global audience. In this book I'll refer to the model as the "*Slicing Pie* method" or "*Slicing Pie* model." Yes, it's slightly more boring, but hopefully it will be easier to understand for foreign audiences!

Risk vs. Theoretical Value and the Term "Slices"

In *Slicing Pie*, the calculations convert the value of contributions to what I referred to as "Theoretical Value" or "Relative Value." In this book and the online calculator, the value is expressed as "slices", instead of a currency to underscore the difference between what's at risk and the actual value of the input. Using a currency, such as dollars, made it seem like the amount somehow reflected an actual value.

It's important to note that a company's value is *not* equal to the sum of inputs. Early-stage startups are exceedingly difficult to value and efforts to do so are generally futile. When the term "slices" is used, instead of currency, people seem to have an easier time understanding that the number of slices is unrelated to the value of the firm.

Theoretical Value and Slices are the same, and the results of calculations that use them are the same no matter what you call them.

Pre-Owned Supplies and Equipment

In the original model I did not recommend applying a multiplier to pre-owned supplies and equipment. I have updated my opinion and now think that the non-cash multiplier (2x) should apply. Risk is being taken and the individual deserves the risk premium.

In the recovery framework, the multiplier would be removed and the cash value would be retained. My reasoning is that if someone was terminated for good reason or resigned for no good reason keeping their money and property could easily be construed as fraudulent behavior. *Slicing Pie* is about trust and transparency.

Facilities

Similarly, in *Slicing Pie*, I wrote that the multiplier does not apply to rents on facilities. Originally, my feeling was that it would be rare that a landlord would provide free or reduced rent to a startup company for a space that would otherwise be leased for cash. In most cases, the space is available because it can't be leased. Therefore, the multiplier would not be fair. However, I've changed my mind on this point because I want the landlords to enjoy the benefits of the risk premium so they will be less likely to kick the startup out of the office when they find a cash renter. The Pie Slicer will apply the non-cash multiplier to rent. This change is similar to the change I'm recommending with regard to equipment and supplies. When the risk of not being paid is accepted, the contributor deserves the non-cash multiplier.

In the recovery framework, slices contributed in lieu of rents are lost in the event of termination for good reason or resignation for no good reason because they are intangible. If the landlord kicks you out without warning they are resigning for no good reason, for example.

Non-Solicitation

A non-solicitation agreement prevents former employees from causing other employees to leave the company for other jobs. This means that if someone leaves a company they can't go back and hire their former coworkers or even recommend them to others looking to hire. This agreement was omitted from *Slicing Pie 2.3* only because I forgot about it. In this book, I recommend that all former employees agree to non-solicitation because I don't believe it's fair to other employees for former employees to lure away the best contributors. I don't think the inclusion of this agreement affects the model in any way, but I think it's important to bring the matter to your attention.

Calibration and Partitioning

When I first published *Slicing Pie,* I had a number of inquiries from people who wanted to use a "hybrid" of the *Slicing Pie* model and a fixed split. There were two main motivators: 1) founders wanted to keep 51% so they could maintain control, and 2) founders felt that early participants took on more risk than later participants. To address these issues, I included the concepts of Calibration and Portioning in later versions of *Slicing Pie*.

I have excluded these concepts from this book because they are not in the spirit of the *Slicing Pie* model. I don't believe that anyone should be entitled to a chunk of equity just so they can maintain control (they can always use profit sharing), or any other reason. I also don't believe that risk necessarily goes down over time. I will likely remove or revise these concepts in later updates to *Slicing Pie* too.

Use the model, as described, and it will be the fairest equity model possible. Any changes will make it less fair.

Loyal Employee Protection

The original *Slicing Pie* book did not provide an outline of Loyal Employee protection as described above.

The End

Thank you for reading, I wish you nothing but total success with your startup endeavors! Please let me know how things go!

I hope your life is filled with delicious Pies!

Special Thanks

Thank you to *The Slicing Pie Handbook* readers who provided edits, ideas and constructive criticism during the development of this book!

Charles Haine
Ronald Hiller
Noam Wasserman

FAIRSQUARE LLP
(a London-based Slicing Pie-friendly law firm)
Maxine Chow
Deborah Griffiths

If *you* would like to be on this list, please provide meaningful, constructive feedback to help improve this book.

Index

Made in the USA
Monee, IL
08 November 2021